Blessings Afforded a Common Man

To LEATHA Many BLESSINGS

Jules J. Hull Jr.

Jules J. Hull Jr.

ISBN 979-8-88851-421-4 (Paperback)
ISBN 979-8-88851-423-8 (Hardcover)
ISBN 979-8-88851-422-1 (Digital)

Covenant Books
11661 Hwy 707
Murrells Inlet, SC 29576
www.covenantbooks.com

Acknowledgments

To my Creator, Lord, and Savior,
His grace and forgiveness make all things possible.

To the true love of my life,
My beautiful wife, Donna, God's greatest blessing.

To my father and mother,
Who loved, protected, nurtured, and molded me.

To my grandparents,
Who led by example.

To the children I have fathered,
And the children I have gained through their nuptials,
The grandchildren their love has fostered.

To all who represent the many threads,
Woven into the fabric of my life.

Introduction

Each of us is born with the ability to reason and make choices. Some will choose wisely, others will not. No one can predict the actions, circumstances, or events that will unfold throughout life. Some believe in luck or destiny. Others say we have a prearranged number, a day we are born and a day we will die. Everything in between that span makes up a life.

Instincts guide us at birth. We cry out, we suckle when we are hungry, we sleep, and we grow. God's first blessing is the gift of life itself. The chance to experience breath, warmth, and touch. Our parents and families protect, nurture, and love us. This is our next blessing in a long list to follow.

This book shares my personal experience. It is a story of growth, my development of faith, and my belief in God. I am extraordinarily common. I have found no cure, and I have no patents and no degree, but I have loved and been loved. I have been blessed many more times than can be counted and more than deserved. I may be the recipient of God's love and blessings, but I have just a small part in the play. It is the recognition of the times I could have fallen, the times I have fallen, and those faithful people God placed in my path. The times that others reached out, loved me, and lifted me up.

As you take in these pages, I hope they may inspire you, increase your belief in God, and help you realize all the blessings in your life.

In the Beginning

The year was 1962, and the month was October. John F. Kennedy occupied the White House, though he would sadly be assassinated thirteen months later.

My parents and their parents all resided in the state of Pennsylvania.

My father was a lineman working for the Bell Telephone Company. My mother was employed as a teller for a local Philadelphia bank. My mother had been hospitalized at Chestnut Hill Hospital weeks prior, due to toxemia brought on by her pregnancy. It was the evening of October 7, and Mom would turn twenty-one the following day. My mother's older sister, my aunt Trudy, worked as a nurse in the hospital. My mother had started labor and was examined by her physician. He told her she would not be ready to deliver for several hours and then went to dinner. Shortly thereafter, I would make my appearance to the world, delivered by my aunt. This was already the second miracle afforded me, as Mom had several miscarriages before my conception.

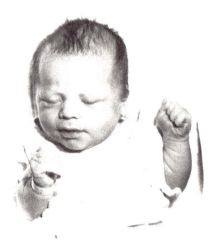

One day blessed

I was the fifth grandchild to be born on my mother's side of the family and the first on my father's. I was blessed to have two loving parents and two complete sets of grandparents.

First Christmas with Grandmom and Grandpop Hull

My parents first resided in a twin home located on Limekiln Pike, in the city of Philadelphia. My earliest memories of the house are of my crib and bedroom. The crib was not only where I laid my head; as a toddler, it would double as my trampoline. A picture depicting Jesus as a shepherd hung on the wall. My grandmom and grandpop Hull resided within walking distance on Woolston Avenue. I have limited memories of their residence. I would guess that I was between two and three years of age.

Grandmom would take care of me when my mother returned to work. This early bond between us was truly special and would last a lifetime. My grandpop was still working at the time, employed by the Philadelphia Traffic Division, repairing traffic lights. I was the proud owner of a red plastic fire engine. It was a riding toy with a steering wheel, a seat, and a storage compartment located in the rear. Grandmom would prepare and place a snack in the rear compartment. I would then get behind the wheel to begin the morning commute, between the kitchen and the parlor. Pulling into my designated parking space, in front of the television, I would sit and watch *Sally Starr* and *Captain Kangaroo*. Later in the day, I would sit on Grandmom's lap, and she would read to me and show me the comics from the paper. At nap time, she would lie on the bed beside me. She would tell me of her plans to move to the country. She planned on planting a large garden and raising chickens and ducks. To coax me to sleep, she would often recite nursery rhymes and sing songs. I can still remember the words to one favorite, "Hi, Diddley-Dum-De. The cat ran up the plum tree. He ran so fast he scratched his ass. Hi, Diddley-Dum-De," and how I would laugh.

"Sing it again, Grandmom," I would reply. This was our little secret, as I was not to repeat the lyrics to my parents, risking the possibility of getting her in trouble.

Grandmom saved her S&H green stamps and purchased me a plastic riding horse connected by four springs to a red metal base. If it was a real horse, I believe I would have ridden it to the point of exhaustion. It is still in my possession, and two more generations have enjoyed time in the saddle.

Grandmom and Grandpop had a dog. Her name was Boots, and she was a Labrador mix. Everywhere they went, so did the dog. I was very fond of Boots, and she was my first animal companion. This relationship and Grandmom's love for animals set up my own passion for future pet ownership.

Grandpop was an avid model railroader. He had a train platform set up in the basement with multiple tracks. It was always a joy when he would take me downstairs and operate them for me. Grandpop always wore green work trousers and a green cap. His face was weathered and coarse, with stubby whiskers. He had smoked since about age fourteen, and his brand was Lucky Strike. A smoking stand always sat beside his favorite chair. I vividly remember smoke suspended in the air mixing with dust, forming patterns as sunlight streamed through the windows.

Grandmom always wore a dress; I never saw her in pants. Grandmom would take me for walks, often to a corner store. There she would often buy me candied cigarettes packaged in a box imitating Grandpop's brand.

Back home, my mother would dress me up like a little man in a button-down shirt, bow tie, and shiny shoes. Some mornings before I had awakened, Dad would stop at a local bakery and pick up freshly glazed doughnuts, usually still warm. I would delight in it as we would share a fresh doughnut and a glass of milk.

Dad, Mom and me as a baby

As this was my world and these were my heroes, I took on their likes and dislikes. My grandpop dunked his Oreo cookies in milk, so I did too. I also ate cream of mushroom soup with saltines crumbled up in the bowl. This was Grandpop's favorite, so it became mine.

Although I spent much more time with my father's parents, we also visited my mother's parents at least every other weekend. They lived in the community of Trainer, located in Delaware County. A melody played from the constant hum of equipment related to the oil refinery in the town of Marcus Hook, located just across the railroad tracks. An odor often hung in the air, and in the distance, an open flame blew out of a pipe elevated high in the sky. The flow of air traffic overhead added to the soundtrack, due to the home's proximity to the Philadelphia airport. A small field separated the back of their residence from the train rails, including a high-speed line. I was warned to stay away from the tracks, a request impressed many times upon me. You could feel the vibration of passing trains inside their house. Their home was a twin, and it had a large side yard.

My mother's father was born there and resided there his whole life. As a younger man, he was very athletic and was offered contracts to play both professional football and baseball. He turned the opportunity down because the games would be played on Sundays. Older family photos depict Grandpop Plummer as handsome and well-built in his younger years. With age, he became portly. He would tease and then hold me at bay in our play interactions, winding me up, and of course, I always returned for more. Grandmom Plummer was loving but stern. My mother's parents both held positions in education. My grandfather was a principal at Chichester High School, and my grandmother taught health and physical education and coached girls' sports at Ridley High. I remember them most often wearing dress clothes. Both were very active in their churches.

Grandmom & Grandpop Plummer home in Trainer

My aunt Trudy, uncle Albert, and cousins Danny and Debbie lived with my grandparents for a while. This provided me with play-mates on visits. Danny and I were the same age; he was born three months before me; Debbie was just one year older. Our relationship was the closest I had with any of my cousins. Mom had two brothers and two sisters. Her two brothers lived out of state, one in Colorado and one in Michigan. When the family was all home, my grandparents would be full of pride and joy.

Every Christmas for my first thirty years would include a trip *down home*, as my grandparent's home was referred to. My earliest recollections of visits include constantly having ticks removed after playing in the field, the orange streaks remaining on my skin after the sting of Mercurochrome was applied to a scratch or cut, and summer holiday picnics out on the screened-in patio. I also once had an actual ride with a dozen other kids sitting atop the hoses of a real fire engine at a neighborhood carnival. Liability would never allow anything close to this in our modern day.

This space in time also provides my first memory of pain. My parents' bedroom was located down the hall at the front of the house. I was running into my parents' room, and tripping, I went headfirst into a cast-iron radiator. I recall crying lots of tears as my mother cradled me in her lap. I remember looking up at the streetlights passing by, as we went to the hospital. I don't remember the number of stitches I was told were needed to close the wound. This would be just the first of many bumps, bruises, and scars I would receive as my young life moved on. I was cared for and loved by all around me. All my experiences were new and exciting. I'm sure God must have watched over me, providing His love and protection, but His power was beyond my ability to understand.

Time with cousins

Off to the Country

My parents, and Grandmom and Grandpop Hull, would both go on to purchase building lots in Berks and Rural Montgomery County (the country).

On weekends, Grandmom and Grandpop would travel to their new property and establish a driveway. Next, Grandpop constructed an outhouse, followed by a one-room shed at the rear of the property. There was no electricity in the structure. Lighting was supplied by kerosene lanterns. The shed, upon completion, was furnished with a full-size bed and a primitive three-burner cookstove, also fueled by kerosene. The building lot was previously a field. Several mature apple trees resided in various locations. We would stay overnight on weekends. I would sleep warm and comfortably between them. In the morning, Grandmom would prepare breakfast, and Grandpop would slowly tame the tall field grass with a push mower. This was a terrific sport for me as I followed behind him and conceived each new path as a maze.

During this same time, construction began on my parents' new home. They had also purchased a one-half acre of land that was also previously a field. Once excavated, there appeared to be more rocks than dirt. Dad and Mom would travel to the property on weekends so that Dad could monitor the progress of the project. On each new arrival, there was plenty to attract and capture my imagination. Piles of dirt lay on the perimeter of the lot, mounded up from the excavation, practically mountains for a child my age. The smell of fresh mortar and lumber lingered in the air. Planks bridged the span between the existing ground level and the new foundation. Studded wall partitions formed bedrooms, halls, closets, and other living spaces. All of it provided a perfect playground to fascinate my young mind. Other memories include my father using the contractor's saw horses to create a table. There we would sit and eat homemade sandwiches with chocolate milk from Longacres Dairy for lunch. Closer to the home's completion, I also remember my mother and father painting and working into the evening, with clamp-on work lights casting long shadows against the white plaster. I have no recollection of anything related to moving; it just seemed as if one day, I woke up and was in my new home.

The next memories that come to mind are of my first playmates, David and Mark, two brothers who lived right next door. Two more brothers, David and Billy, lived just across the street. We all grew up together, playing football and baseball, riding our bikes, and sledding in the winter.

I recall looking forward to kindergarten and being excited about riding the bus, which turned out to be a yellow van. Once at school, the day would include being served warm cartons of milk and graham crackers, wearing an oversized shirt specified for finger painting, and nap time lying on individual mats. The playground at kindergarten contained an old-style sliding board, a merry-go-round, monkey bars, and swings—all without any of today's modern safety precautions in case of a fall. On the television, *Speed Racer* was my favorite cartoon. Attending six different school buildings over the years, most of this class would remain together and graduate high school some thirteen years later.

My parents were members of a small Methodist church, and I remember attending Sunday school and vacation Bible school. We sang songs, completed crafts, and were taught stories of Jesus on a child's level, and the basis of my faith began. My parents also taught me a children's prayer that I recited back to them before bedtime most every night. "Now I lay me down to sleep, I pray the Lord my soul to keep. If I should die before I wake, I pray the Lord my soul to take." This would be followed by "God bless Mommy and Daddy, Grandmom and Grandpop," and so on. My life to this point was simple and without care.

The year 1968 would mark a significant change in my family. Mom's belly had begun to grow, and I was told she would be having a baby. That July, my new baby sister, Sherri, would arrive, ending my status as an only child. I remember being taken to the hospital by my grandparents. At that time, the hospital was located on Charlotte Street in the town of Pottstown. This was so I could wave to my mother looking down on me from a window on the upper floor. Hospital rules allowed no children to visit. I had anxiously anticipated my new role as big brother, but she seemed to cry too much and needed a lot of attention. Our age difference would separate our interests and friends as we grew up.

Mom and Dad showed no favoritism, so no dynamics really changed. I enjoyed playing with the neighborhood kids and did so at every available opportunity. When playmates were not present, I entertained myself by building with blocks or using my matchbox cars outdoors in a sand pile. I was a junior engineer, constructing bridges, tunnels, and roads. I spent a lot of time and imagination on doodles and drawing, having been introduced to the craft by my father.

Summer soon ended, and it was time to start the first grade. At some point between the first and second grades, your level of status was already being determined by your peers, based on your kickball ability, your personality or lack thereof, and probably your hairstyle and clothing. Once you were assigned your ranking, it would stick throughout your school career. I sported a crewcut, prompting the nickname "bald eagle." I was also often among the last chosen for anything to do with athletics. No need to feel sorry; I learned to cope, and there was no need for therapy.

Second Grade

I moved on to the third grade and was now attending an older four-room school building. I had formed my opinions about school, and in my mind, each day carried the drab necessity of the previous day. By this point in time, I already looked forward to the weekends. Saturday was a day to rise early, as cartoons occupied the airwaves till noon.

Early in the fourth grade, I met a boy in my class who would become my best friend. He was thin, with blond hair and blue eyes. His name was Stephen. His family had been farming the land for generations. Steve was the oldest of four and already had responsibilities, unlike most of the other kids (me included). He was assigned chores and would help his father before the start of his school day. He invited me over one Saturday afternoon to play. This would be my first introduction to an actual working farm.

Mostly everything on the farm depended upon the weather and necessity. I have always thought that if more kids had the opportunity to spend a summer on a farm, the world would look much different. There were so many things to do there that I don't recall ever watching TV on a single visit. There were forts constructed from straw bales in the barn. We played tag, hide-and-seek, baseball, and football. In the winter, we went sledding, built forts in the snow, and had snowball fights. We ran and played in the fields surrounding his home. I can honestly say the very best times and most vivid memories of my youth are of a friend and his family's farm. It provided us with a constant source of clean wholesome fun and adventure. I consider this period in time, as well as the opportunities and memories it furnished, to be a gift from God.

Rebel with No Cause

Life was good as the transition from child to know-it-all began. I approached the age of twelve, starting junior high in a newly constructed building complete with a planetarium. It was built with large open floor plans versus the traditional classroom setting. By this time, my circle of close friends had expanded, and I had spent equal time with my friend Raymond.

Ray and I often stayed overnight at one another's house. He lived with his mother and stepfather. Ray's mother worked while his stepfather held no job that I can remember. The stepfather drank, often in excess. He was purposely ugly to Ray with no cause while praising me for no reason. It was uncomfortable, and I often felt bad for Ray's situation. Ray was much more flamboyant than Steve and much more outgoing than either of us. He was always upbeat and encouraging. Three was never a crowd, and we always got along. There were never fights or major bickering among us. One could not have asked for two better or more faithful friends. When everything seemed against us, we were each other's support system.

No one in my circle shared many classes together, as it was a large student body combined from several elementary schools. I enjoyed reading and science. I also enjoyed taking shop and art classes. The art teacher would sign my hall passes in advance, and I would go to the art room instead of the study hall. I started to attend school dances as they were held. This would be my only extracurricular activity pertaining to school.

By this point in time, I had left the Methodist church. I didn't have any friends there, and I didn't feel like I fit in. I had attended vacation Bible school at a nearby Lutheran church, and Stephen and his family were members. Coincidently, our neighbors attended the church also. They offered a weekly ride, so with the transportation problem solved, I split from my parents' direction and went on my own.

I liked the independence, and I was glad my parents allowed it. The pastor had previously been a chaplain in the navy, and his wife had been my first-grade teacher. Shortly after beginning attendance there, I started confirmation classes to learn about church history and doctrine and to become a member. I also participated in the youth group and was active in retreats and any other events offered. Pop culture would also play a role in this time period. Television, movies, and songs would affect how we dressed, what phrases we used, what we thought, and even how we may have behaved. I often had girls on my mind, searching for and imagining nonexistent relationships in my head. I looked forward to any time spent with friends.

I continued to have close relationships with both sets of grandparents as I matured. I noted there was a stark contrast between them. My mother's parents traveled on many occasions, even seeing Europe and the United Kingdom. They attended separate churches. Grandmom was Baptist, and Grandpop was a Methodist. Both were very active in the life and events of their individual churches. Their choice of different denominations was odd to me, but it was their arrangement, and it worked for the fifty-plus years they shared together.

They were also active in their community. They often did things independently of one another. My father's parents lived closer to our home, and I was able to spend much more time with them. They did everything together. I do not remember them going on any type of vacation. They did enjoy a nice Sunday drive. I very much enjoyed being in their company. I would stay overnight at every opportunity, over the summer months, for weeks at a time.

On warm July and August evenings, we would sit on the back doorsteps. When younger, I captured lightning bugs and enjoyed listening to tales of their younger years. Unfortunately, these were their memories, and other than bits and pieces I can remember, most of their history is lost to time. I helped my grandparents with plantings, cutting grass, and trimming back the blackberry patch. Grandpop had constructed several coups to house my grandmother's livestock. I helped feed and haul water to the chickens and ducks.

Grandpop was inventive and creative. He was a ham-radio operator and had a collection of calling cards from others like him all over the world. It was always a big deal for me when he would queue up the mic and let me talk. He also had a complete basement workshop, including a table saw, drill press, grinder, and sander. This would not be unusual, except all the tools were designed and built by him, using used motors, belts, and pulleys. He was the family electrician and TV repairman. I was right by his side on many occasions as he disassembled the back of the television and removed and tested various tubes.

My father's parents did not attend church, except for family occasions. My grandmom contributed to shaping my faith by displaying her own. She said her prayers daily. I would listen to her speaking in whispers. She told me that when she was younger, she would have dreams and premonitions of things. She explained that it scared her, and she prayed for it to stop. It was, and still is, my belief that she had a close relationship with God and that she was blessed. I loved my grandmother dearly. My fear of disappointing her helped me in a lot of my decision-making. We could talk about most anything, and she treated me like an adult. In my opinion, none of her other grandchildren ever experienced, or appreciated, the wealth of love and knowledge she had to share.

During this time in my youth, an apparent power struggle began between my mother and myself. I was ready to stretch my wings while she put constant time restrictions on any outing with friends. My playtime revolved more around daylight than the hands on a clock. This would result in constant disagreements and groundings. My father would often take up my case and argue on my behalf, resulting in friction between my parents. I was not near ready to leave the comfort of my parents' care but longed for the day I could.

The seasons changed, and I spent as much time as I could away from home. The farm was a constant source of fun and refuge. In the summers, I would sometimes help bale hay as, on the farm, work came before play. In our leisure, we would shoot bottles and cans at a dump in a nearby patch of woods. We swam in a spring-fed pond, having battles, piling the algae on inner tubes, and throwing it at one another. In the winter, we would make forts in the snow, have snowball fights, sled, play ice hockey, and ride a snowmobile. I still remember taking off our wet clothes and enjoying the warmth of the coal furnace in Steve's basement. At church, Steve and I were confirmed and officially became members of the congregation. Shortly after the confirmation, my parents also switched churches, following me and becoming members.

Age thirteen was on the horizon, and my focus turned further toward girls. I enjoyed music and had long believed in the words and stories depicted and sung through love songs. Hollywood also long knew the perfect storyline: boy meets girl, followed by a wonderful romance leading to marriage and happily ever after. There was a lot of crash and burn to get through before anything close to a romance would materialize. The eighth-grade storyline ended with "better luck next year."

As I entered the ninth grade, I would soon turn fourteen. We were told that we needed to choose the tenth-grade courses that would affect our career path. I wasn't sure what I wanted to do the following day, let alone the rest of my life. I had a really encouraging art teacher, and it was my favorite class. I decided teaching or something to do with art would be my goal. The students were assigned advisers to help determine a direction, mainly based on grades. Behind door number 1 was an academic career, door number 2 was general studies, and door number 3 was a vocational school, also considered the bottom of the food chain. Against my adviser's advice, I chose to sign up for the academic course of studies.

That summer, my mother enrolled me in a conservation project at the junior high nature trail in the morning. This was followed by each afternoon spent at the public pool. I rode my bike to the first location, came home for lunch, and then pedaled off to swim. That summer at the pool, a brief romance bloomed and was managed by showing off my swimming skills, holding hands, and sitting on my towel next to her. Better for the experience and bragging rights, summer ended along with the relationship. With that, it was time for the first year of high school to begin. In our school district, two separate junior highs purged their ninth-grade students into one tenth-grade student body. I would turn fifteen just over a month into the school year.

It was now time to laser focus on my majors, popular music, girls, and fun with friends whenever possible. I knew what was expected and the difference between right and wrong. I would have to say, during this point in time, I kept Jesus in my closet along with my Sunday clothes. I was happy to share every Sunday morning with Him and put Him back when the church had ended. By the end of the first quarter, I was failing in biology and algebra. Why on earth would anyone want to substitute letters for a perfectly good number? It just didn't add up (pun intended).

By the end of my second quarter, it was painfully apparent that I had chosen the wrong door. I didn't take this opportunity to seek advice from God or even my parents, but I spoke with Steve. He was disillusioned with the curriculum and decided to switch it up and head to vo-tech. I changed my courses from academic to general for the remainder of the year and limped along, setting my sights on the eleventh grade, turning sixteen, and driving.

Steve had taught me to operate a manual transmission in his father's truck in the safety of an open field. On occasion, I would operate one of the farm's tractors. At times, Stephen's father would have us fetch a tractor and wagon from some fields he rented miles away from the farm. I would follow behind him in the truck with the flashers on. My dad would also let me get behind the wheel occasionally between church and home. The confidence he displayed by letting me drive always made me feel like a grown-up. Steve's cousin, Carl, was the first of our gang to get his driver's license, so he was also granted the title of honorary chauffeur. Next was our friend Christopher, followed by Stephen. We all played in church league softball, and even at that level, they designated two teams, from the same church, just like the pros and their farm team. Nothing had really changed since first-grade kickball. No problem. We were all together and having fun. We hung out at assorted pizza and sandwich shops. At times, we sat on the banks of local streams, passing the day fishing. We spent time playing cards and frequented the mall and arcade.

I met a girl at a dance sponsored by the Lutheran Conference at an Allentown college prior to the start of my junior year. We danced and exchanged some kisses and phone numbers, and I was finally *going with someone*, the official term for a steady relationship at that time. She was from a different school district, twenty minutes away from home. This provided additional incentive to obtain a driver's license.

At that time, you could apply for your driver's learner's permit months prior to your sixteenth birthday. School didn't interest me half as much as knowing the state driver's manual inside and out. To obtain your permit, all that was required was to correctly answer questions that pertained to laws and information contained in the publication. I aced the test on my first attempt and, with that, was on my way to freedom and the responsibilities that went with it.

Dad was all for me having a driver's license and a car, but of course, Mom was not. Dad once again argued on my behalf and won. He found a used car in the newspaper for $400. This would drain my meager savings of birthday and holiday money put away over the past fifteen years for college. It was a dark-green 1968 Ford LTD two-door sedan, the perfect starter car for a young man with discerning taste. Other kids were driving Mustangs and Camaros, but it was paid for, dependable, and it was mine. Our deal was that I would maintain the car, fill it with gas, and pay the insurance. I detailed it weekly and changed my own oil. I added an FM converter, connecting it to the AM radio under the dash.

Washing my first car

I was beginning to feel like an adult. With a learner's permit in hand, I drove it, with Dad as copilot, several times to my girlfriend's house for a date. He would return at a designated time to pick me up again. Two weeks after I turned sixteen, Dad and I traveled to a DMV drivers' center located in Norristown, and I passed my driver's test.

The eleventh-grade year had already started, and I was about to discover what was in the package I had picked behind door number 3. You would attend your home school for half of the day for classes and vo-tech for the other half to learn your trade. Steve had picked electrical and was assigned an afternoon slot. I selected plumbing and would be bused there in the morning. I knew not one thing about the trade but realized it was a profession that would always be needed.

A perception existed among many students at home school that vo-tech was where they sent all the hoodlums and future felons. Most had the attitude that all the students were just attending to get out of regular classes. It was a different environment, and there was a definite hierarchy to contend with. I wasn't afraid of a fight, but I wasn't looking for one. Even though I was a first-year student, being a junior put me into second-year status, which offered some protective benefits.

I very much liked the class and the instructor. He was an older man, retired from the trade, kind but stern. If you crossed the line, he would physically and literally put you in your place. He had the respect he deserved, and I admired him. The seniors were still not afraid to take a chance on foolery when the opportunity allowed. The plumbing shop contained a C-shaped locker area, and centered in the space was a large round commercial sink called a Bradley, named after the manufacturer. The game was to cover the drain with multiple paper towels and fill the basin with water. Then those involved would pick up an unsuspecting first-year student and place them in the sink. I remember one such incident.

A student named Troy was the intended victim. He was from another school district. I didn't know much about him at the time but noticed that he seemed focused and eager to learn the trade. It was three-to-one as the seniors grabbed him, in their attempt at indoctrination. Troy was not about to go in without a fight. He punched, kicked, and twisted to avoid their endeavor. The best they could accomplish, as I recall, was to partially immerse one leg. One might question how this story might relate to blessings in my life. Troy's path and mine would intertwine again some five years later, and eventually, he would marry my sister, Sherri. Happy ending, yes, but to this day, there is still a dispute between us over my alleged involvement in the earlier stated covert operation.

The school year continued, and by January 1978, my first romance had ended. There were plenty of fish in the sea, so I moved on and focused on happier topics. Our church congregation would gather to present a series of comical skits before the beginning of Lent. Named the Fastnacht social, it provided light entertainment, refreshment, and fellowship prior to the start of the solemn season. I was at a rehearsal for the planning of the event.

I was given a part in a skit opposite a cute younger girl I hadn't noticed previously. Chemistry was at work as we practiced our roles. We started to date, and weeks later, she accompanied me to my junior prom. Her family was great. She had two married adult sisters, one married adult brother, and one adult brother still at home. I felt welcomed at her home and enjoyed the family interactions. She was very mature, and at fourteen, she would start the family meal prior to her parents' return from work. Sometimes we would babysit her young nieces and nephews. I was happy to sit by her side every Sunday at church. We spent as much time together as parents, work, school, and each day would allow.

My junior year went by quickly, and summer soon arrived. I focused on my relationship and continued to support my habits of dating and car ownership by working at a fast-food chain. My senior year was about to start. With no skill set, I decided to try out for the soccer team. I enjoyed the practices and the running, and soon I found my place on the team. My most frequent position for games was the bench. I think it all relates back to the whole first-grade kickball conspiracy. Anyway, I was better for the experience; I got a lot of exercise and got to wear a team jacket with my name on it. While participating on the team, I would also meet another future brother-in-law, Michael. He was younger, upbeat, and fun to be around.

There was some bad news as I returned to the vo-tech. Our instructor was ill and would be taking the year off. A substitute teacher was brought in, to take his place. I found the class to be a waste of my time now, as he had no experience in plumbing whatsoever. I decided to take advantage of a work program and took a closing shift at the restaurant. This was advantageous in several ways; I made extra money, wasn't expected to work weekend hours, and best of all didn't have to report to school until noon. My course load was light, and I enjoyed my classes and instructors. I made the honor roll twice, something I had never accomplished before. I had a steady girl, a car, and a job, so life was good.

Senior year passed by ever so quickly. The class traveled to Disney World on a senior trip; this would be my first flight on a plane. Upon our return, almost everyone looked forward to the upcoming prom. The school year was over before I knew it. I graduated and set my sights on finding a job in my trade and continuing my romance. I was young and willing to bend the rules and twist the dial on my moral compass. Although I listened to the sermon at church each Sunday, I seldom considered the message.

4

Change of Seasons

Youth passes by so quickly. You are praised for good behavior as a
child, and signs of maturity begin to bloom. The world is still small;
you are somewhat self-involved and don't realize how quickly life is
changing around you.

High school was behind me; it was my time to be responsible
and take my position on the treadmill. The year was 1982. Both
pairs of my grandparents were aging before my eyes, yet I hardly
noticed. Grandpop Plummer had been hospitalized for some heart
issues. He continued with some medication, exercise, and dietary
changes. I don't recall any major health problems for Grandmom
Plummer, except a slight head tremor. I remember my dad making fun of the turntable full of various prescriptions and medications at arm's reach on their kitchen table. Grandmom Hull was on
blood pressure medicine. Grandpop Hull often had coughing fits.
Neither of my father's parents ever had a stay at a hospital. One day,
Grandpop Hull coughed so badly he must have expelled some of the
by-products from a lifetime of smoking. It shook him up, and he
quit smoking straight away. I still remember the sound of his breathing. I watched as his level of daily activity slowly waned. Grandmom
would call when he needed help with anything outdoors. I took over
the lawn-mowing responsibilities and whatever else was asked. I was
happy to oblige. Grandpop would often sit in a lawn chair and watch.
Soon after, he was diagnosed with emphysema.

It was a beautiful Saturday morning in September, and my dad told me to make sure I went over to see him. Grandpop had gotten oxygen to help ease his breathing. Someone had told him, "Once they bring in the oxygen, it's all over." He must have taken this as gospel. He seemed down, so I tried to lift his spirits. I kissed him and told him that I loved him. I then went on my way, thinking I would see him again in a day or two.

There was a double date planned for that evening, and we headed to a movie theater located in the town of Pennsburg. I was not sure where we ended up following, but somehow, I got word to get to my grandparents' house right away. Upon my arrival, I was greeted with sorrow. My life, as I knew it, had changed forever. This would be the first pain I would experience as someone most honored and loved left my world.

I tried to go about my normal routine following his passing. Work helped to alter my focus slightly. The evening of his viewing arrived, and I struggled to breathe. I even took a prescribed sedative to calm my nerves. Attendance was light at best; my grandparents only had a small circle of friends and family. My behavior bordered on hysteria as I looked at him lying in that casket. *"That's not my grandfather!"* I exclaimed as I wailed. The man I saw lying there was clean-shaven. His face was not weathered; it was now pale and chalky. His hair was combed back, there was no green cap, and he was dressed in a suit and tie. I am quite sure I intensified the grief already present in the room. I could not be consoled. I even noticed Grandpop Plummer had teared up over my despair. He was buried the next day, and now I had nothing to do but go on.

Initially, after Grandpop's passing, my uncle spent several nights staying with my grandmom. Grandmom was uncomfortable being alone as she hadn't been without my grandpop since their wedding day. I had never even seen her drive a car. They had done everything together for fifty years. When my uncle went back to his normal routine, I took over the watch. I was happy to be with her, as I had always felt more closely bonded with her than with my own mother. We talked and we consoled one another. Grandmom was a big television-evangelist watcher, and she told me that Grandpop had raised his hand at the end of one such broadcast and asked for God's forgiveness and to be saved. This seemed to give her at least some peace. Life continued moving forward, and time marched on.

My reactions to the future passing of loved ones have lessened in intensity, but they still bring me great sorrow. I have come to understand that death is natural, and it will come for us all. I have accepted that God has an order and a reason. It is a part of His plan, not for us to judge or understand but to continue our faith and obedience to Him.

Grandmom and Grandpop Hull in a rare formal

5

CHAPTER

That Thing Called Love

Love—the most powerful of all human emotions. It has existed since the beginning of time. It is God's greatest gift. We all possess a desire to give it as well as to be its recipient. Love can both wound and heal. It is a subject portrayed in books, movies, and songs. If you have found your true love, it is a treasure like no other. Love's favor benefits both young and old and knows no boundaries across race or creed. We first receive love from our family, but as we grow, we wish to share it with others.

I remember being attracted to girls as early as first grade. I partnered with a girl for square dancing in the gym. Those girls were sure hard to figure out. Fantasy inclinations came and went. Brief encounters, such as holding hands while roller skating, were a rare treat. Movies and television make it all look easy. Real life, however, is much more awkward and embarrassing. Junior high dances offered the first real opportunity to be in the closest proximity of the opposite sex. Immaturity and inexperience would rule the night. Songs of love played through the loudspeakers, enticing you as you sat at the room's perimeter. Perspiration would increase as you gathered the courage to ask any random girl to dance. You push forward on your mission, sometimes dealing with the sting of rejection, feeling as if every eye was upon you and celebrating your defeat as you returned to your seat near the corner. The process is endured and repeated, with each small victory building your confidence.

Brief relationships and romances ensued till the magic age of sixteen. It may have been a growth in maturity or freedom a driver's

26

license afforded. 1978 would be the year the words *I love you* were first exchanged between a girl and myself. We confided in one another and shared our secrets and insecurities. We dated each other for over three years. By this time, she was a junior, and I had graduated. It was all wonderful, and everything was just as I had pictured it, until it wasn't. Slowly, the relationship changed and eroded. We broke up for a short time and then reunited. I don't remember all the causes of our decline, just hurt and emptiness. The final split came early in 1982, when we parted, vowing to remain friends. It was truly the lowest point of my nineteen years. I felt gut-punched and alone. I still longed for her company but faced my new reality. I had been out of school for almost two years. My job and social life didn't bring me in contact with girls. I had no path I could think of to escape my loneliness.

One day, the image of a girl I had previously been introduced to at a church youth function just appeared in my mind. She had attended as a guest of someone else. I remember that she was attractive and seemed nice. I no longer recall how I was able to contact her. We went on a few dates, and I took her to meet my grandparents. She was very outgoing in their company, and I got the wink of approval from Grandmom. When my grandfather passed, she was there for me and shared in my sorrow. Her family was much smaller. She had one older sister. Her father seemed uninvolved. She was very close to her mother, and the three of us did many things together.

I entered the relationship way too quickly, with my past love still fresh in my memory. I am sure that she sensed this, which caused her doubt and suspicion. All my family and friends liked her. I escorted her to her prom, and we double-dated with some of her friends and mine. I spent more time at her house than I did at my own. She graduated near the top of her class and planned on furthering her education. The school was located close to home. She would stay at the dorm and be home on the weekends. Her studies were very intense. Somewhere in this period, we got engaged. It seemed then that happily ever after was around the corner.

Following the announcement of our engagement, we had set no date. Nothing within our relationship changed, though I felt ready to move forward. I acted poorly regularly and gave her reason to doubt me. She was forgiving, but shadows had been cast and would remain. The relationship may have still worked, but our pathways kept seeming to separate. The catalyst always would lead back to me. I was selfish and inconsiderate in a big way. During this time, a chance meeting would change my life's direction forever.

It was a Saturday afternoon in the late summer of 1984. I was at my parents' house, just hanging out alone. One of our adult neighbors had a younger brother attending college. He was across the street at their residence for a visit. He had created a video recording for one of his courses. He had come to our house with some friends and wished to use the VCR to show his presentation. Included in his group of friends was a girl named Donna and her boyfriend. I knew Donna as the secretary at the plumbing company where we were both employed. I was truly surprised to find her as part of the group at the front door. My first introduction to her was when I filled out an application for employment. I still remember glancing at her while waiting for my interview.

I considered her very attractive on my first impression. She had long, dark brown curly hair and pale blue eyes. Her contours and proportions matched perfectly. She dressed very professionally in a blouse with a nice-fitting skirt and wore high heels that accentuated her figure even more. She walked very gracefully, and her voice was soft and feminine. I wondered why she chose to work there. I thought she could have easily been a model. The other conclusion I reached at first sight was that she was off the charts and out of my league. I pictured her in the perfect relationship with someone on the fast track, way better than myself. Opportunities at work to have any interaction with her were limited. I knew very little about her. I noticed she owned and was obviously able to drive a manual transmission. That told me she was spunky, and I admired that.

Other than a brief good morning and a smile, my only other chance to speak to her had been once during a lunch break. On that occasion, we had a small chance to find out a little more about one another. We spoke a bit about our current relationships. Our conversation was brief and soon interrupted. She seemed to show an interest in me. Since we were both otherwise spoken for, I just attributed it to her politeness. On this day, however, she was in my house, sitting on the hearth of the fireplace. I tried hard not to be apparent as my gaze was upon her while the video played. This was the first time I had extended time to focus on her. I had not seen her dressed casually previously, and I was not disappointed.

The video ended, and after some small talk among the group, I was invited back across the street for a game of volleyball. Donna occupied the opposite side of the net, which allowed me more time to observe her without being so obvious. I teased and gently flirted with her when our positions directly opposed one another. I got her to laugh several times, and she had such a great smile. Soon enough, the game ended, and she left with her boyfriend. It was time to go back to our regularly scheduled lives. That would probably have been the end of the coincidence for most people. However, I was still intrigued and could not shake thoughts of her from my mind. The odds that this attractive girl would somehow end up in my house were zero to none. The odds that she would break up with her boyfriend to date me were zero to infinity. I was committed and engaged; my future was spoken for by my own doing.

With no reason to look any further, I contemplated the multiple bad decisions I could make. Foolishness and fantasy ruled my thoughts, and I looked upon her as an object. Something placed on a high shelf, beautiful to look at but hard to reach. I knew her last name and that she lived in Pottstown. I figured out her address using an earlier form of the Internet, the phone book. I was curious and decided to see where she lived.

Some days later, I drove past her house to find it was on a long driveway and could not be seen from the road. This experiment netted me nothing. I decided to return after dark, hoping to catch a glimpse of her. My heart beat quickly as I nervously walked up her driveway in the cool evening air. I took notice of her parked car and hoped that was an indication of her presence. Looking back, it was stupid on a scale I had not achieved before. (Okay, so now what? Walk up to the front door and knock? "Yes, uhhh… I um… just happened to have been in the neighborhood, so I thought I would stop by and say hello." Sure to leave a lasting first impression on her parents.)

Scared but anxious, I continued to a lighted window. Mustering all the nerves I had left, I cautiously peered inside. There I saw her standing in her bedroom, wearing a pale-yellow nightshirt. As I continued my observation, she made a motion, like a dancer in ballet. She gently swung her arms and raised them above her head, first to the left and then to the right. She looked so beautiful; her movement was so fluid and so graceful. She turned off the light, and the show ended. I rushed away quickly, feeling ashamed as if I had betrayed her. I was consumed with what I had witnessed, and it only served to magnify her appeal. Her image was permanently etched in my mind. I vowed not to repeat my performance but to become more noble in my endeavor.

Over the next few months, I lived a lie as I continued with my current relationship and dreamed about another that didn't exist. At work, I was still treated to a glimpse of her, an occasional smile, or good morning. In some way, I needed to find an opportunity to speak to her without scaring her away. One warm fall afternoon, I finished work early, and I knew the route Donna followed to travel home, so I pulled my car into a church parking lot and anxiously waited for her to pass. I followed behind her, keeping a distance. The Lord must have smiled upon me because she stopped at the local mall. I hung back until she parked her car and proceeded to pull into the space beside her as if by chance. I'm sure I surprised her, and I knew this approach could easily backfire. I decided that this was a time for complete honesty, with a little finesse.

We exchanged niceties and small talk. I tried to gain further information about her relationship. I gently confessed my feelings for her. She seemed a little uncomfortable, and I tried not to push. We parted for the evening, with my hopes high that the slightest spark had been lit. At work over the next few weeks, I was anxious and felt painfully awkward the few times we made eye contact.

Soon Thanksgiving arrived, immediately followed by deer-hunting season. Everyone in the shop except my crew partner, Phil, and I took a few days off. Donna was left in charge of the office and schedule. On the Monday after the holiday, Donna gave us our job assignment and some homemade chocolate chip cookies. That gesture, along with her smile, conveyed at least some further curiosity from her. I began to feel more at ease as if I had a chance to be with her.

The new year approached, and on its eve, everyone worked a half day. It was decided among the crew that we would meet at a local elementary school for a game of touch football. Donna expressed interest and was invited along. I offered for her to get there by following me, as she didn't know the location. I explained to her that I had planned to make a quick stop at Ames, the local department store in Boyertown before the game. This would also afford me some time alone with her. We parked our cars and walked together toward the store entrance. It felt so good just to finally be alone with her and walk by her side. At that moment, under the clear blue sky, I turned to her and uttered the best line I could come up with: "Why don't you start the New Year off right and marry me?" I know what you are thinking. I had just swept her off her feet, and we never made it to the game, opting instead to find a local justice of the peace. But that's not what happened. Instead, she laughed nervously and rolled her eyes. Donna didn't run for her car, so I took this as a further step in the right direction. I am pretty sure I did gain entry into the Guinness book of best proposals, with an assist for the most romantic location. We arrived for the game, and my anticipation and confidence were at a new high.

1985 started with the true realization that I was being dishonest with my fiancée and myself. I knew the engagement needed to end, and I wrestled with my conscience. Soon into the year, Donna and I had exchanged phone numbers and contacted one another regularly, spending hours on the phone line. There were a lot of highs and lows as I tried to navigate my reality.

Just as it seemed Donna was ready for a new commitment with me, doubt would pull her back. I proposed a day together, just to talk in person and learn if this was all more than infatuation. We decided to meet at her house and drive to a shopping mall located in Montgomery County, some distance away. This was to ensure we would have some time alone and not be discovered by anyone we knew. It was a cold January morning, and several inches of snow had fallen the night before. I was not to be deterred under any circumstances and headed to her residence. She introduced me to her mother, and then I escorted Donna to my car, opening the door for her.

There was no awkward silence as we traveled toward our destination, finding endless topics of conversation. I was immersed in the absolute delight of being with her as we continued our journey. We parked the car, and I asked if I could hold her hand as we walked to the mall entrance. Once inside, we walked about, talking, laughing, and holding hands. Hours had passed, but it seemed like minutes. I leaned toward her, and she met me halfway to share our first kiss. When our lips met, I could not describe the torrent of emotion that engulfed me. It was a true culmination of endless thoughts and desires, all in one electric moment. We shared one more and then another. We left and headed home; my hand locked in hers the whole journey back. We reached her driveway, and I dreaded parting with her. We shared embraces and some much deeper, soulful kisses.

I was completely intoxicated by her beauty, warmth, and being. This was a whole new level of magnetism. In that moment, I was sure what I felt was far beyond infatuation. I expressed to her my intense desire for a commitment and to have her to myself. I vowed to break my engagement and end my existing relationship. I asked Donna if she could do the same. I was willing to step away from what was safe, sure, and expected. I would trade it all away because of the total delight of just one day spent with Donna. I told Donna that I could manage to share her for Valentine's Day, but I wanted to be the one by her side on her twenty-first birthday early in March.

The following day, I broke off the engagement. I had loved her and still had feelings, but it was more than obvious my devotion was far less than needed for a marriage. I tried to be gentle, but it was very difficult and brought tears. It was the hardest thing I ever had to do. I knew if the relationship continued, it could only end under far more painful circumstances.

Soon afterward, Donna and I started to meet each other after work in a church parking lot along her route home. My every day was wished away, all but for those brief moments with her. She was not as immediate with her breakup, taking more time to process how and when. Although very eager to be her one and only, I was careful not to push and let her take the time she needed. Finally, she made her decision, and we became a couple. Just as I had wished, we would be together on her twenty-first birthday. I had a plan to add an extra special touch to her day. I had set out early with several homemade painted signs wishing Donna a happy birthday. I stationed them at strategic locations, from her driveway all the way to work.

Donna with homemade billboard on her twenty-first birthday

Donna's mother had contacted me and said she had planned a surprise party for her. It was my part of the plan to occupy Donna and arrive with her at the prearranged time. It was unknown to me prior, but this occasion would also be my introduction to her whole family, grandmothers, aunts, uncles, and cousins. I sat by Donna's side as she opened cards and presents. I wasn't as nervous as I had anticipated, and I felt accepted. Wanting to express to her the true depth of my feelings, my birthday gift was a promise ring. It was white gold and had a tiny diamond chip. I was overjoyed by her reaction as she slipped it on her finger in front of everyone.

Beside Donna, as I hoped for, on her twenty-first birthday

Over the next few weeks, the full focus of my attention was on Donna. She was the breath in my lungs, and I was truly in her orbit. I am not sure how I even focused on anything related to work. At any moment together, I would take every opportunity to press my lips to hers.

Happy to press my lips to hers

Some mornings we would meet early at a diner and have break-fast together before work. Our relationship had an extra level of mystery and excitement, as we kept it a secret from our coworkers. We continued to grow ever closer, discussing our thoughts, hopes, and dreams. We shared everything, and I felt welcomed into her family. I was her choice, and they felt no need to second guess it. Donna's mom was a dedicated wife and mother, and I soon felt I was included in that dedication. Donna's father seemed quiet, but he often thought of something funny to say, adding to my feeling of acceptance. He, too, shared a devotion to his wife and children.

I soon realized that Donna had been named for both her father and mother and found that to be unique. I learned that her mother had hand-made most of her dresses, blouses, and skirts. I met her younger brother, David, who seemed to have an affinity for tinkering with motorcycles and trucks. This would later lead to him becoming an excellent mechanic specializing in Power Stroke diesel engines. My attraction and affection for Donna intensified, quickly turning to love. I was certain I had found my soulmate, and Donna became my best friend and confidant.

We soon discussed marriage. I wanted her to know how much she meant to me, and I tried to make every moment together amazing. My father and I drove to the jewelers' row in Philadelphia. He took me to the shop where he had purchased my mother's engagement ring years earlier. I searched the displays for a ring I felt worthy of placing on her finger. On a mild spring day, only six weeks past her twenty-first birthday, I took Donna for a walk in Valley Forge National Park. I told her I was ready to replace her promise ring and asked her to marry me. I was never more sure of anything I had ever desired in my whole life. She teared up, and without any hesitation, she said yes.

Please pause and take a moment to consider all the obstacles in my path, yet despite myself, she said yes. You cannot force love, and I must exclaim truly that God's blessings were upon me. We returned to her house and announced our good news to her family. There we were greeted with excitement, joy, and anticipation. My parents, however, expressed doubt and skepticism over the pace at which we were proceeding.

Shortly thereafter, on a visit to my maternal grandparents, Donna faced an interrogation from my grandfather, uncle, and my father. They noted the difference in our religions. Donna was a Catholic, while I was a Lutheran. I had been attending Mass every Sunday with Donna since we started to date. The service was almost identical to the Lutheran service and, if anything, was more solemn. My future wife was very devoted and had great faith in God. This would lead me to examine and be more serious about my own devotion. We left the occasion angry, and some time passed before we spent any significant time with my family.

Engagement photo captured by Donna's father

I spent every available moment by her side. I would follow Donna home from work each day, where her mom would make dinner for us. I enjoyed any occasion to be in the company of her mother and father and believed they were the perfect example of a great relationship. The household had a distinct harmony, and I felt that I had also become part of the symmetry. We had set a date in May of the following year and jumped right into planning our wedding. We focused all our attention on the many details. We quite innocently would fall asleep together every evening. Somehow, I would manage to wake up each night at 3:00 to 4:00 a.m. so I could return to my house. One of her mom's only rules was that I could not spend the whole night, but apparently two-thirds was acceptable. Even the interruption of sleep was more than worth it to spend additional time together.

Work continued, and I advanced to operating a truck with my new crew partner, Troy. He offered his encouragement and was truly delighted for us. Troy was the only person at work with whom I shared our plans. I continued to find ways to impress Donna and make her smile. Recalling one such event, Troy and I cut grass at the shop. I knew Donna would glance out the window as we worked, so I made a cardboard sign saying *"I love you!"* and held it up on each pass of the riding mower. I found such joy in her smile and laughter. The summer continued, our love increased, and we enjoyed every moment we spent together. We pulled our funds together, paying off our cars and saving money for a house.

Maybe there was something in those love songs and movies after all. I felt I had a star's role in the greatest romance that ever existed. Perhaps God had just provided me with all the ingredients for a perfect recipe.

Meet Me at the Altar

We had selected May 24, 1986, as our wedding day. If a year could go fast and slow at the same time, this span of our lives certainly did.

We set about making all the arrangements for our special day. We compiled a list of family and friends that we wanted to invite. We reserved our date with the church and signed up for premarital counseling. We visited several locations with Donna's parents to hold a reception. We contacted a soloist, a DJ, a florist, and a baker. We decided on the members of our wedding party and picked out tuxes. Donna and her mother selected fabric for the bridesmaids' gowns. That's right… Fabric. My future mother-in-law was an extremely talented seamstress. She insisted on making not only the bridesmaids' gowns but Donna's wedding gown as well. She was thrilled beyond words as she absorbed herself in the endeavor. Her dedication and love through this gift made our wedding plans much more special. Right from the start, I felt especially connected to Donna's mother. Her love for her children was obvious, and I felt a special comfort and inclusion in her company. I knew I had arrived right where I was supposed to be.

Special moment with Mom

Donna had purchased numerous books and magazines on weddings. The content was organized, and she had a binder full of all the related pertinent information. We sat on the living room floor many evenings, going over details and addressing invitations.

Six months before our day, we set about looking at real estate, taking Donna's parents along for guidance and advice. We settled on a twin home we could afford in Pottstown.

Our first home on Hanover Street in Pottstown

We made some minor improvements and went about acquiring furnishings. Our possessions at the time were mostly a mixed bag of hand-me-downs and thrift store finds. Amid planning our future, news of our relationship finally leaked out at work; it was bound to happen. Nothing specific was ever said, but I think behind the scenes, management did not like the idea of Donna and I being a couple. After an exchange between one of the owners and myself, I was sent home. At this point, I felt it was best that I move on to further employment. Months prior to our wedding date and without any new position lined up, I gave my notice. Fortunately, through God's good grace and our friend Glenn, I was immediately hired by another plumber, Ray. Once again, I was employed. Things in the office also eroded for Donna, and soon after my departure, she also found a new position at an insurance firm.

The months of our planning were complete. Finally, the night before our wedding arrived. The wedding party gathered at the church for our rehearsal and attended the rehearsal dinner afterward. Our guests departed, and Donna and I shared embraces in complete contentment with one another. After sharing our last kisses of the evening, we parted and tried to sleep, waiting for our wedding day to arrive. I spent the evening in our new home, where I had been living by myself for about a week. I arrived the next morning at my parents' house to greet my groomsmen, dress, and complete the final preparations before heading to the church. I waited in a room behind the altar with Steve, who was my best man. It was a beautiful day with blue skies and plenty of sunshine. The church slowly filled with our guests as my anticipation increased. I was excited and ready to profess my conviction and love for Donna in front of all our friends and family.

All our guests were seated, and our mothers were escorted down the aisle. The warm sunlight shone against the church, illuminating the stained glass as I stood in my place at the altar. The music began to play as the groomsmen escorted the bridesmaids down the aisle. Everyone stood and turned as Donna and her father entered the aisle. The music began again as he escorted her toward the altar. Donna appeared radiant, more beautiful than I had ever seen her before. Her wedding gown was truly stunning, a testament to a mother's undying love and devotion to her daughter. Finally, she arrived by my side at the altar. Her cousin Dorothy, our maid of honor, set about arranging her train.

The priest greeted our guests and asked Donna's father, "Who gives this woman to be married to this man?"

Her father replied, "Her mother and I do."

He then pulled back her veil, kissed her, and placed her hand in mine. I smiled the biggest smile in all my twenty-three years, and we turned toward the altar. The priest leaned toward me and said, "She was worth the wait." We kneeled as the priest spoke and prayed over us. We stood once again and faced one another. We repeated our vows to one another before God and all in attendance. Every word was absorbed into my heart and into my soul. I rejoiced from within as we were joined as one. We kissed, and our guests applauded as the priest announced us as husband and wife. Never had a day produced the joy, love, and pride I experienced on the day of our union. I walked my new bride down the aisle to greet everyone who had shared in our moment.

Mr. & Mrs. Jules Hull Jr.

We returned to the altar for pictures, and before we arrived at the reception, we obtained permission from a local family estate to take more photos. It was a beautiful setting, and Donna's parents had taken photos at the same location on their wedding day, making it even more meaningful.

A perfect day

We arrived at the reception hall to the applause of our guests as announcements of the wedding party were made. We enjoyed the meal and were more than happy to kiss whenever someone chimed their silverware on a glass. I hadn't previously envisioned much of our reception except for our first dance. We danced to the song "Heaven" by Bryan Adams. The room went dark, and everything around us disappeared. For a moment in my mind, I was alone with my beautiful bride, dancing to our song and so very much in love.

Our dance ended, and the fun began. We were very careful in selecting the DJ, and he did not disappoint. Around 95 percent of that crowd was on the dance floor for the duration. He was truly gifted at entertaining, playing the perfect combination of old and new. Donna's family definitely knew how to have fun. We formed a train to the song "Locomotion" and went about the dance floor, the room's perimeter, and even in and out of the restrooms. Later, we joined arms and formed a kick line to Sinatra's "New York, New

York." Everyone was having such a good time that my father-in-law paid the DJ to play an extra hour. The party showed no signs of stopping, so at the end of that hour, the DJ offered to play one more hour for free. This was one of the best days of my life, and its memory is as fresh as the day it happened. Finally, it ended, and many of our guests stayed to fold tables and chairs and assist in the cleanup. Donna and I went to spend our first night together in our new home. Exhausted, we crawled into bed and fell asleep in one another's arms.

We arose the following morning and made a stop at our favorite diner. To our surprise, we were joined by Donna's mom and dad. We enjoyed talking about all the fun we had on our wedding day. We thanked them for all they had done to make it so very special. We said our goodbyes and left for our honeymoon in Florida. We looked forward to our lives together and all the blessings we had yet to experience.

Mom and Dad with us on our wedding day

That Thing Called "Life"

We returned from our honeymoon, anxious to see our families. We went about opening wedding cards and presents and writing thank-you notes to all who had shared our day. Although I had only been employed by Ray for a few months, he generously paid me for the two weeks we had been away. We were thankful for the opportunity to have started out in our own home versus renting an apartment. We liked our new residence and enjoyed the charm of an older property. Donna set to housekeeping and enjoyed arranging furniture and keeping things in order. The house was large and had plenty of room to start a family. We picked out our first child at the SPCA. She was a little black puppy with a white patch on her chest, a mixed breed but favoring a German shepherd. We named her Lady, and just like Boots in my youth, she went everywhere we went.

Breakfast with baby Lady

We now had responsibilities. Life was busy; there was no big drama and no tragedy, and we both worked. We invested time in small home improvements. We enjoyed one another and spent time with our families. We really liked our first home and may have been content to stay there but for a few issues. Our adjoining neighbors proved to be just plain unpleasant, and the parking was limited on the street causing a situation that continued to be a problem. We spent our first Christmas together as a married couple. We discussed our options again with Donna's parents and decided it was time for a change. A builder whom Ray worked for had purchased some building lots along a rural road and out of town. It seemed like a step up we could afford, so we purchased a lot. The building contractor's home plan was bi-level. We chose this because of the additional living space the design afforded us. We thought we could save additional money on the home's price because I would install the plumbing and heating myself. Ray was always kind and allowed me additional days to work at the house when he could. Many long days ensued, and both families helped with the project. Finally, settlement arrived, and we moved into a brand-new home.

Life was normal again; there was no big drama and no tragedy, and we both worked. We still invested time in home-improvement projects like building a deck and a shed. We continued to enjoy one another and spend time with our families. The furniture we had started out with soon showed signs of wear. We discovered antiques and enjoyed searching for them. We slowly replaced some of our furnishings with them. God blessed us, and we were content. Although we had responsibilities, this was a wonderful and mostly carefree time. Life together was new and happy each day.

Several years passed, and we decided to have a child. Everything went according to plan, and we had no trouble conceiving. The only complication of the whole pregnancy was my poor wife's delicate stomach. She seemed to have morning sickness in the morning, noon, and night. She dealt with it the best she could, and we had tremendous support from our families.

Along this part of our journey, my employer, Ray, would mentor us again. He had my full respect and had become like an older brother. Ray suggested we go to a birthing center for prenatal care and delivery. Ray explained that hospitals were for sick people and that babies had been born throughout the ages without them. The idea appealed to both of us and made perfect sense. Our child wouldn't come into the world in a cold, sterile environment but instead be delivered by midwives, surrounded by family in a warm and inviting home. Donna continued with her workload in what seemed like a constant state of nausea. We completed our courses on childbirth and went for prenatal visits. As there are so few surprises in life, we decided not to find out the sex of our new baby.

Months went by, and finally, Donna went into labor. We packed her bag and headed to the birthing center, apprehensive and nervous. Before the age of the cellular phone, we contacted our parents. We wanted them to be present to share in the blessing of our baby's arrival. And so it began, the miracle of birth. A child turns and slowly passes from the womb to the birth canal. I stood beside my beautiful wife, drenched in sweat, more naked than clothed, panting, moaning, and crying—all natural, with no drugs of any kind to ease her pain. I held her hand, wiped her forehead, and stroked her hair. I prayed for her pain to subside and for our child to be born. Her labor continued as the pain intensified. They drew her a bath, and she lay in a clawfoot tub, soaking in the warm water. She was so strong and so brave.

After twenty-three hours of labor, she was extremely exhausted and losing her strength to push. The crown of our baby's head was clearly visible. One of the midwives brought a mirror and held it so that Donna could see the baby. They persuaded her to make one final effort. Somehow, with all her might and crying out, she pushed once more. Finally, our child arrived. I touched our new daughter for the first time as I cut the umbilical cord and placed her in her mother's arms. Completely spent from her efforts, tears rolled down her face as Donna held our child. Tears of joy filled the room from those in attendance (Donna's mother, her aunt Carol, and my mother and father). God's greatest gift and largest blessing just came into the world. We named our new daughter Rebecca Elaine. New titles were given to those present. (Father and mother transformed into grandfather and grandmother; husband and wife transformed into father and mother). Donna rested, and by noon, we were home.

Mommy, Daddy and newborn, Rebecca

I was stuck in the '60s and insisted that my new daughter wear cloth diapers. Troy was our first visitor, and while holding our new baby daughter, he was christened. He never complained and wore it like a badge. My choice of diapers was overruled shortly after that.

Mommy, Daddy, and baby were doing fine. We were content; life together was new and happy each day, except now, with limited sleep. Bills seemed to accumulate quicker than before. Donna and I had discussed her staying home with our child long before it was a reality. She felt her parents had sacrificed and appreciated her mom staying home during her childhood. The antiques we had collected seemed out of place in our new home. We could no longer park in our garage, as it was full of workbenches, power tools, and related materials. I wished for a basement or some type of shop.

We discovered Donna was pregnant again three months after becoming parents; so much for natural family planning. Welcome but unexpected news. After a visit to our physician, it was determined that her due date was on our daughter's birthday. One more of life's unexpected surprises. Time moved quickly, and our new child was visibly growing. Donna juggled our baby daughter, returning to work part-time and again endless nausea.

It was a Friday afternoon in June, and Ray was on vacation. I was assigned to check the phone messages on the tape machine and feed the animals in his absence. After completing that, I was on my way home when I spotted a real-estate sign in front of an older brick home. A detached garage connected to a small barn was located at the rear of the property. I immediately noted the property address and wrote down the realtor's phone number. I quickly headed home. Excitedly, I described the property to Donna. We contacted the realtor straight away and set up an appointment for six o'clock that evening.

We met a realtor named Wendy and did a walk-through of the property. Now keep in mind that we were living in a home that was not yet three years old. Our existing house had every modern convenience. Here we were, touring a property left in an era bygone. Many of the rooms had paneled walls or dated wallpaper. Almost every room had staple-up tiles on the ceiling. One-half of the dimly lit basement utilized wooden pallets as a walkway across a dirt floor. The electrical system consisted of several dated fused boxes and antiquated knob and tube wiring. Original oil cloth covered some of the upper floors. The kitchen and bathroom were both in true need of updates. I could tell by Donna's expressions that her thoughts were the same as mine. We completed the showing, and as we traveled back to the current time period, our comments were mostly negative. The differences between our present residence and the one we had just toured were too numerous to count. It was hard to even consider moving my pregnant wife and infant daughter to a home we felt needed so much updating.

Saturday was our next happy day. The bills were piling up, and the birth of baby number two was one day closer. We visited Donna's mom and dad and told them about the property. We discussed our finances and Donna's desire to stay home with our children. We noted the difference in the values of the two properties and that the value of our existing home was higher than the older property we had just looked at. Taking that into consideration, this would provide additional funds we could work with to start remodeling. It also seemed to be more rural and in a desirable location. We contacted the realty office again and set up an appointment to visit the property on Sunday afternoon. This time, Mom and Dad would accompany us. Wendy, the realtor whom we had toured the property with originally, was unavailable, and it was a shared listing, so we met a different agent named Randy. That meeting kindled a friendship that has lasted to this current day. Randy has since provided me with employment and has offered insight and advice. He has been a trusted confidant and has lifted me up in prayer. We once again arrived at the property, this time with Mom and Dad at our side.

Our Home in Oley

On this visit, we took more time and noted potential we had not observed during our first viewing. We looked at everything more objectively and thought more about what could be versus what was. Mom and Dad offered positive insight and advice. Mom always had a gift for removing herself personally from an equation and giving an objective opinion. This time, we left the house excited with a brand-new perspective and a new plan. We made an offer contingent upon the sale of our present home. The gentleman who owned the property was a widower and had recently remarried. His new wife lived a short distance away, and they did not need the upkeep and expense of two properties. Our offer was accepted, and we listed our home. Now all that had to happen was a couple of nibbles and a bite, and we would be off to a new adventure.

Months passed, but the nibble never came. We were awash in disappointment. We had hung all our future hopes and dreams on making the property our new home. We were very anxious and worried that someone else would purchase the house. Eventually without a buyer, the contracts on both properties expired. We listed our property again, praying everything would work out… And then it did. We had a buyer in several weeks. We promptly renewed our contract for our desired home. It was amazing how much stuff we had accumulated in just over three years of marriage. The job of packing began, and items were boxed and stacked in our garage.

Finally, within weeks of Donna's due date, moving day arrived. It was Thanksgiving weekend in 1989. Instead of fighting Black Friday shoppers, we started moving in. Both families arrived to help load and transport our belongings. Our friend Glenn, a manager with Reading Foundry plumbing supply, arrived with the company's steak body delivery truck. Donna's brother, David, brought a large trailer, and in addition, we had three pickup trucks and our parents' passenger cars. We managed to pack and load everything and made the move in one trip.

After my father's passing, I found a video he shot depicting the whole event. Having fun with it, he made it in a documentary style with comments and interviews. With his video camera, he toured the house room by room, including the exterior and the barn. It is now a cherished recorded memory, as the house and property now appear much different than they did back then. It also contains my father's and mother-in-law's voices recorded. Now deceased, it is a comfort to hear them. Like an army of ants, everyone worked together to unload and place our possessions in their designated rooms. While very pregnant, Donna carried, loaded, and lifted. Windows were cleaned, and dishes, linens, and towels were unpacked. The living room, bedroom, kitchen, and bathroom were all set up and ready for use. To our surprise, the gentleman we purchased the home from filled the oil tanks. Both of our families returned on Sunday, December 3, to celebrate our daughter's first birthday two days early.

We were still moving items around and living out of boxes on December 8. Ray kept me close to home, knowing Donna was due any day. I was working for some nice folks nearby, remodeling their kitchen. Coincidently, their son would also be born that year, and our children would become friends. Donna called and said she was going into labor, so I quickly headed home. We gathered her things, called our parents, and headed for the birthing center. Since her first labor had taken so long, I took my time, even stopping at a convenience store for some snacks. I was scolded when we arrived, as they expected us much sooner. Donna was examined and already well-dilated. The midwives quickly attended to my wife's needs. Family members gathered for the birth, and none too soon. Our new son wasted no time, making his way on the journey through the birth canal.

Jules III first day of life

I honestly have to say, Donna's length of time in labor would reflect each child's personality. My daughter, growing up, was always cautious and reserved. Always watching, she made decisions after much thought. My son, however, has always been full of energy. Jumping in feet first, ready to act upon his thoughts and emotions. Once again, we did not find out about our child's sex ahead of time. I had a feeling that we were going to have another daughter. This being said, we did not come to any agreement on a boy's name. We went home soon after the birth, with our son unnamed. The next day, which was Saturday, Ray and his wife, Bonnie, stopped by to congratulate us, meet the new baby, and see our new home. The solution for our nameless baby came from Ray. He simply said, "You must name him Jules. How could you name him anything else?" So with that, our son became the third to carry the name. And, once again, each new happy day and sleepless night began with a new baby who was colic, crying at the top of his lungs. The only way to console him was to put him in the car in the middle of the night and drive till he fell asleep.

This was our new life—working during the day, attending to the children, and any extra time left devoted to transforming our new house to suit our desires. First on the list of projects to be completed were a new kitchen and bathroom. As if we did not have enough fun activities to choose from, it was shortly after that I began to contemplate starting my own business. I had long done side work after hours. It has been the path taken by almost every tradesman as they transition to being out on their own. It was something I had been thinking about for quite a while. We thought it would provide a way for Donna to be home with our children. We, of course, discussed it with our parents. Donna's parents were understanding and offered encouragement. My parents thought my timing was foolish and irresponsible. I also discussed it with Ray. He too offered me encouragement and understood my desire. He was also thoughtful as he would allow me to return to work for him if things didn't pan out. I bought a used one-ton pickup truck and installed work bins and a pipe rack. Donna's father painted my name and phone number on the bins, and I looked official.

My first work truck, lettered by Donna's dad

Plumbing suppliers, Reading Foundry and Boyertown Supply both extended extra credit, allowing me to stock my truck. The managers of both establishments passed out my business cards to anyone who stopped in and needed a plumber. In the early days, Ray offered me work when I did not have a full schedule. And so with that, I was off and running—the same career but with new management. I was a husband and father of two, taking on the challenge of remodeling a sixty-year-old property.

We were not looking to change the charm of our home's time period. Our goal was to update and have some modern conveniences. The remodeling went on for years, pretty much the whole of our children's youth. Many of their pictures as toddlers show them poking their heads through holes in the walls or sleeping in rooms with open wall cavities.

Growing up with construction

We put so much of ourselves into the renovations that our house became like a third child as time passed. The home's transformations were all created from our thoughts and desires. My wonderful wife was literally by my side, assisting me on every project. Demolition, wiring, plumbing, drywall, and painting—you name the task, and my wife, soft and feminine, had been my assistant, working with me as my equal and my partner, exerting herself like a man.

Over the years, Donna and I each have had a reoccurring dream with the same premise, that we have moved and dislike the home and new location. We have lived here for thirty-one years, and the property has truly changed from house to home. We raised our children here and welcomed their friends. Our family and friends have gathered here on many occasions. Tears have fallen, and laughter has been shared. There are countless memories within its walls. This dwelling has provided us shelter and has kept us warm and dry. It is simple and quaint, and I am proud to be its keeper. Close to its centennial and curious about its past, I had the title searched. Coincidently, I have worked for or have been acquainted with a relative of every one of its previous owners. I have acquired a photo of each of our home's former occupants. We have occupied our home longer than any prior resident.

When we moved here, we were among the neighborhood's youngest residents; now, we are among the oldest. Many of our original neighbors have passed on, taking their knowledge and memories of our village with them. It was a pleasure and a privilege to have known every one of them. I hope someday that perhaps a grandchild may occupy this home in my place. I wish that whoever may occupy it will experience the love, memories, and blessings I have known while I was its steward.

Check the Box

I wish to impart this story of God's good grace after my son recently reminded me of its significance.

It has no date that I can recall. My children were most likely ages five and six. My workday had ended, and I pulled my work truck into our driveway. I have a spot aside from the garage where I park it each evening. At the edge of the spot lay a large appliance box. I had intended to cut up the cardboard for recycling. Being the end of the day, I thought I might blow off a little steam and just do the stupid, what guys are generally capable of. I thought it might be fun to drive right over that big old box. I applied a little pressure to the gas pedal, my fender right up against the cardboard, pushing it slightly forward.

A sudden vision of my children playing inside shocked my senses. I immediately turned off the ignition, flung open the door, and jumped from the truck. The screams of my children confirmed my premonition. I grabbed a child under each arm, breaking down in tears as I ran with them toward the house. I sobbed as I explained to Donna what had happened. We quickly examined the kids, checking for any signs of injury. Images of a tragedy, that somehow and in some way, had instantly been averted. At some point later in time, my children related to Donna their version of the event. They told her that they had held the truck back by pushing against the inside of the cardboard.

See it however you may, but it is my firm belief that God once again provided His loving protection upon my family.

Generations

Time is in constant motion moving forward. The pages of life begin to yellow, wrinkle, and tatter. The opportunities, events, and lessons life can offer are much the same. It becomes apparent and expected that grandparents will someday expire. I am blessed to have witnessed the love, faith, wisdom, and shared experience my grandparents passed down to me. Our grandparents had all lived through the Great Depression and World War II.

Wedding Day - Grandmom Good pictured left
and Grandmom Forster pictured right

Wedding Day - Grandmom and Grandpop Plummer
pictured left and Grandmom Hull pictured right

By this point in time, my number of grandmothers had increased by two through marriage. My wife's maternal grandmother, Grandmom Forster, had been widowed since 1972. She was cared for and looked after by all her children. She was always witty, and she often spent time with Mom, Donna, and our children. Her memory had started to fail, and she passed away in 1992. I was happy for the time I had shared with her. I still had one grandpop, my mother's father. No apology for his previous poor judgment of Donna was ever offered. I could tell, however, through his interactions with my wife, that he had realized his mistake. She was loved and treated as any other granddaughter. My grandparents celebrated their fiftieth wedding anniversary with a gathering attended by their children, grandchildren, and loved ones. They experienced the joy of becoming great-grandparents.

The head tremor that plagued Grandmom Plummer had gotten worse, and she began slipping into dementia. She became more than Grandpop could take care of and was placed in a senior facility where she could receive proper attention. I am sure her absence caused him some guilt and great heartache. He was hospitalized, and Donna and I traveled to see him. During our visit, he appeared fine, perhaps a little down. We talked, wishing him well, hugging him, and telling him we loved him. He passed away on October 21, 1993, just eighteen days past his eighty-fourth birthday. I have always felt he just lost the will to go on. Grandmom Plummer lingered on until August 1996, when she passed away at the age of eighty-six. My father-in-law's mother, Grandmom Good, passed away in June 2003 at the age of ninety-one.

Donna and I kept up on the lawn maintenance for Grandmom Hull since we had been engaged. Grandmom eventually got weeping sores on her legs. It seemed she was no longer able to care for herself. She seemed weak and disoriented. This would lead to her very first hospitalization. Ultimately, a decision was made to sell her residence. My father had promised my grandfather that he would always care for her. My father began plans for an in-law addition to his residence. Much of my Grandpop Hull's radio equipment and tools were sold. Grandmom could not bear to part with most of her possessions, so they moved them to the basement under the addition. Her bedroom suite, given to her as a wedding present, was passed to me. Donna and I are still sleeping in the same bed that I occupied during overnight visits in my youth. Grandmom moved in with my parents, and I watched as the household dynamics changed. Grandmom spent most of her time in her quarters by herself. I always made sure I visited her at any stop to see my parents.

In time, old memories were repeated, and other tolls of age began. My parents could no longer provide for her needs, and she was placed in a care facility located on Charlotte Street in Pottstown. The building was the former location of the Pottstown hospital. She resided there, first using a wheelchair and then becoming totally bedridden. In time, her memory of what, where, and who vanished, and any conversation ceased. I continued to visit but never as often as I should have. Time marched ever forward. In 2009, my grandmother passed on at the age of ninety-seven, in the same building where my sister had been born.

For as long as I can remember, she has been my greatest positive influence. I did not mourn as I thought I would, instead choosing to be thankful. She lived a full life, mostly without affliction. She had been released from the bonds of her body, and in heaven, she could be vibrant, young, and with my grandfather once more.

Gainfully Employed

I have been blessed to be employed with no significant loss of wages between positions since high school.

Looking for my first full-time job after graduation, I attempted to follow my trade path of plumbing. I was hired by a mechanical contractor who installed sprinkler systems and did large commercial projects. I was basically hired for the summer and spent most of my time at the shop. This consisted of inventory, cleanup, groundwork, and occasionally running parts to mechanics in the field. I was young, able, and ready to start at the top. The few times I had the opportunity to be on job sites, I was often out of sorts with my older, more experienced coworkers. The old shop foreman said I would be laid off come winter, and I wasn't going to wait around for that, so I quit.

My then girlfriend's brother-in-law, George, was operating a dairy farm. He offered to hire me till I found something permanent. He was quiet, very kind, well-mannered, and patient. Coincidentally, our paths have crossed many times, since he later worked as a plumber, eventually starting his own business. We are still friends today, and I have also gained the friendship of his sons.

I had been on the farm for less than a week when I answered an ad for a position at a local family-run dairy. This job allowed me to gain experience, confidence, knowledge, and several friends I have today. I was also started above minimum wage, and overtime was available. Only three months after graduation, immature and still green around the gills, I was thankful for the opportunity the job afforded me. It was 1980, and jobs were hard to come by, especially for someone young and inexperienced. It was also only ten minutes from home. I was hired to operate a machine that formed cartons and then dispensed the milk into one-half pints through one-half gallons. It was interesting and required some skills for setup and maintenance as well as production.

Soon into my employ, I was moved to a different machine that dispensed milk into quart-and-gallon returnable glass bottles. Following that, I was taught to run the pasteurization process, separate the cream from the milk, and follow formulas to make mixes for ice cream and soft serve. My boss was kind and patient. He was also accessible. I was treated well, and along with learning, I gained maturity. Time passed and I decided to move on to a different avenue, so I took a position with a large company that trimmed trees away from power lines. I gained experience and knowledge. It was outdoor work; thus, you were exposed to the elements, insects, poison ivy, burs, and briars. Once again, I didn't feel I fit in well with my new coworkers. Three months after being hired, I was laid off.

While filling up my car with gas, a younger friend, Alan, whom I had known throughout my youth, pulled up to the pump across from me. He had also attended vo-tech. We exchanged niceties and caught up briefly when he told me he had started to work for a small plumbing company. He further explained that they were looking to hire. I stopped by their office shortly thereafter and filled out an application. I was interviewed and hired in short order. I took a cut from my previous wages to fill the position, but I felt it would be worth it to gain experience and actually learn the trade. Obviously, I didn't know it, but this job would change my whole life and alter my path forever. It was a family business, and I was their fifth hire, not including the secretary. All but one of the employees were in my same age group. The company was owned by two brothers, with some backing from their father. It was being run out of the garage of the eldest brother. They had two trucks with full utility bodies; each crew consisted of a mechanic and a helper.

As I was the last hired, the fifth man floated, as was needed between the two crews. I washed vehicles and did ground maintenance. I was not deterred by any of my tasks, realizing they were growing. I was happy that they made sure I received forty hours each week. Once again, I had pleasant, confident employers. The '80s housing boom had started, and they had contracts with several local builders. They had also purchased a building lot, on which they had plans to build an office and a shop.

Many of my early days of employment with them were spent clearing the lot of small trees, bramble, and brush. The knowledge gained from my last position came in handy as I now spent a lot of time with a chainsaw in hand. It wasn't long before my wages increased, and I was making my previous pay. Soon a third truck was purchased, and I was made a helper, assisting a mechanic. It was good work free from monotony, as almost every day we visited a new job site. We worked as a team, always striving to do our best and, once again, acquiring new knowledge, skills, and confidence. I didn't realize it as a young man, but my trade carried over into so many others. I was learning things that would not only make me a success at work but also in my own life and as a property owner.

Things continued to go well, and soon I graduated to mechanic status, operating my own truck with a helper. Troy had been hired, and we were placed together. He and I just clicked. We shared almost identical likes and dislikes in music, movies, attitude, humor, morals, you name it. We made a great team. Troy was extremely eager, and we worked hard and got it done.

A younger version of me at work

We shared personal details about our lives and got together after work as well. Actually, almost everyone got along, and we all went to parties, concerts, and roller skating with one another.

Assorted members of the plumbing crew

That company would eventually spawn seven new companies, myself included. And amazingly, all the relationships we formed are still intact. Thirty years later, we are still friends and even occasionally network together when one of us needs a hand. Unfortunately, or rather fortunately, things would change, ambitions, jealousies, and personalities would prevail, and the good times would eventually end. My reasons for leaving were because of my sharp tongue, a difference of opinion, and my relationship with Donna.

I moved on to work for Ray. He hadn't been working for himself for too long, but he had an opportunity to provide the plumbing for a whole community of townhomes that he couldn't turn away. I was his first full-time plumber. Of all the people I worked for, Ray was the most generous. He would take time to sit down with me and listen. Sometimes we would meet for lunch, or after a long day, he would sometimes buy me dinner. He was always trusting and easygoing. I felt that he took a genuine interest in me.

After my first week with him, he went over some particulars of my work, showing me how he wanted it done. After that, I was mostly on my own. He provided me with a helper, and beyond that, unless I had a problem, I didn't see him till payday. That trust was probably just as important to me as it was to him, and I would in no way betray it. He ended up being much more like an older brother than a boss. He molded and refined me further, providing me with more knowledge. Eventually I ended up telling Troy about him. Soon Troy also met with Ray and began working for him. Troy too was soon on his own as well. He worked on one development or project as I worked on another. Ray taught us boiler installation and wiring the controls. We also did air-conditioning installations, expanding my capabilities even further. There was so much work that, for years, Troy and I worked every Saturday just to keep up.

Eventually I felt I needed to move out on my own, and Ray even helped me with that. Of anyone with whom I ever had the privilege of employment, he offered me the most, not necessarily monetarily but through his care and his willingness to teach. Everyone with whom I was employed passed on to me their skills and knowledge. The lessons and abilities I have acquired have allowed me the capacity to cross over into other trades.

I have not only been able to make a living but also saved myself and other family members from many of the costs associated with owning a home. As I reflect on all the places, the countless hours of work, and the many friends and relationships formed because of my trade, I can't help but look down at my two hands and fold them together, praising God for the gift of knowledge and necessity that He has provided.

In Sickness and in Health

We all face adversity in our lives, probably one of the greatest being diseases. It is most often an enemy unseen. It attacks us from within, weakens us, and erodes our resolve. Sometimes, sadly, it removes us and ends life's journey. I faced an illness, and although unpleasant, the experience yielded gratitude, peace, and a new awakening to faith and God's great love.

A short number of years into marriage, I gained significant weight. I assumed it was a combination of my wife's good cooking, second helpings, and heredity. I'm sure my lack of nutritional knowledge also played a role. I settled into my new physique, uncomfortable with myself but not pursuing any alternate avenues. A case of kidney stones led me to see a urologist. I was told the stones were too big to pass.

The doctor suggested lithotripsy. He explained this procedure as being far less invasive than surgery. He explained that the patient would be placed in a large tub of lukewarm water. Shockwaves would then be used to target and break up the stones. It all sounded relatively simple. What I was not told was that I would be naked, placed in a sling, lifted by a small crane, and placed into the tub. On top of the embarrassment of my nudity, I was told if I was any larger, I would not be a candidate for this procedure. It was not particularly pleasant, and a catheter was also involved, but I got through it without any complications. Following this incident, it was time for a change. I consulted my physician, altered my diet and caloric intake, and began exercising.

With some newfound discipline and encouragement from my family, I soon started losing weight. My mother-in-law was especially sympathetic and supportive. She never missed an opportunity to compliment me on my progress. Eventually I lost almost fifty pounds. I set my sights on a more muscular body. I ate clean and worked out with weights regularly. I gained some muscle but could not seem to achieve my desired goal. I would turn thirty-three in October of 1995. Life seemed to be moving along smoothly. I was happily married, was a father of two children, and had steady employment. I was hardly interested in a birthday celebration. To me, it was just another day. Donna's mother insisted we get together and arranged a small family party. It was a pleasant evening, and Mom delighted in any gathering of her family.

October 17 was a beautiful fall day. The air was crisp, and the leaves had started to change. I had a small remodeling job in the Boyertown area. It was a little late, and because of the time of year, it had already started to get dark. The property owner stopped by to tell me that my wife had contacted her and was trying to reach me. I called home to find Donna frantic. She said something had happened to Mom and that we had to get to the hospital immediately. I packed my tools back onto the truck as quickly as I could and rushed home. A neighbor watched our children, and we sped to the hospital. Donna cried, saying that Mom was gone. I consoled her, explaining that there could be no reason to think that. We arrived at the hospital and were directed to a room where Dad and other family members had gathered. We wept and embraced one another as the gravity of sorrow weighed upon us. Mom had passed away quite unexpectedly with no visible sign of illness. She had come home from work, complained of being tired, had dinner with Dad, and then sat in her favorite chair. In one brief moment, her light and love were taken away, and darkness and despair filled the void in their place. We turned to God with questions instead of praise.

The sun rose the next day, and we shed more tears as we faced the prison of time without her. We had both lost a mother. Her passing affected Donna deeply as she struggled with depression. I wrestled with my own despondency, knowing that God's plan often differs from ours and that some questions will remain unanswered. Time provided distance but not healing as we continued to grieve. Eventually some signs of hope were revealed. I had a dream one night in which Mom appeared to me most vividly. She smiled at me and said that she was all right and that I was not to worry. I woke up the next morning and shared my encounter with Donna. A feeling of peace had settled over me that I hadn't known in months. Still Donna struggled with her loss. Sometime later, a very spiritual friend, Ginger, told Donna that a vision had appeared to her. She told Donna that Mom was happy in heaven, and it was her assignment to help children crossover into the kingdom. Mom completely adored her grandchildren, and this sounded like a perfect position. Each of us was fortunate enough to have known her and to look back fondly and remember the love she poured upon us.

As time went by, Donna's depression worsened. She experienced panic attacks and, on some days, could not leave our bed. This continued until a work injury I sustained turned from bad to worse. My leg had split open at the shin while removing someone's water heater. The wound had been stitched, but it would not heal. I began trips to a wound care center and tried to maintain a work schedule.

One day, Troy and I had work planned about forty minutes away. As we worked, a severe headache came upon me, and a pain in my groin started to double me over. I felt so ill that I had to lie down in our truck, while Troy finished the job. We left and Troy drove me directly to the Pottstown hospital, where we met Donna. I did not have an affiliation with the hospital. My sister-in-law, Lynn, worked there as a nurse and ensured I was assigned a doctor with whom she had great confidence. Blood work revealed both strep and staph present in my system, and the infection had spread to my lymph nodes in the groin.

During his examination, the doctor asked me if I had been using steroids. When I replied no, he then went on to explain that I was physically displaying many of the signs related to Cushing's disease. A medical reference at the nurses' station was made available to me. As I looked through the publication, I became aware that I could be the poster child for the disease. Cushing's disease is usually caused by a tumor on a lung, kidney, or in the pituitary cavity. This causes the body to overproduce the stress hormone cortisol. It can be present in horses and dogs, and most veterinarians are familiar with the disease. Physicians are introduced to the disease in medical school but often never see a case. Before pursuing any solution to the disease, the infection had to be treated.

Prior to diagnosis of Cushings

I was prescribed intravenous antibiotics. Cellulitis set in, and the leg swelled to almost twice its normal size. As a patient, I chose not to waste my time sitting and watching TV. It was during this time that I picked up some art brushes and a watercolor set. I passed the time by painting, which later led to some small recognition as an artist. Once the infection had cleared, my doctor focused on the complete healing of the wound. This was accomplished by wearing a compression stocking, which increased the blood flow across the shin.

I met my endocrinologist, Dr. Jeffrey Freeman. He arranged for further testing to determine the source of the disease. He referred me to another doctor in the Jefferson Health System in Philadelphia. After several months of visits to the city for scans, testing, and repeated bloodwork, we decided on a direction to combat the disease. It was determined that the source of the disease was stemming from the pituitary cavity. I was given two choices for treatment. The first was to use radiation on the pituitary cavity. I was informed that this course of treatment could eventually harden the blood vessels leading to the brain and, later in life, could lead to a stroke. The second option was surgical, using the nasal passage to reach the brain cavity and access the master gland.

The doctor described two scenarios for this approach. One would be like removing a stone from a peach, in which case the pituitary tissue would remain still, allowing for function of the gland. In the second scenario, the tumor would be laced throughout the gland, similar to vanilla fudge ice cream, in which case the whole gland would need to be removed. If this was the case, I would need to take synthetic hormones to mimic pituitary function to the other glands. Adding to the complexity of the surgery, blindness was a possible outcome due to the proximity of the optic nerve.

After prayer and discussion with my wife and family, I opted for the surgery. No actual tumor was found, so the surgeon removed the whole gland. The procedure went pretty much as described. There was a severe headache, and I saw things in a black-and-white haze for weeks. As they removed the pituitary gland, they began administering hormones to replace its function, including hydrocortisone. I gained significant weight, was lethargic, and suffered severe mood swings.

Further testing ensued, leading to the discovery that I was still producing the hormone ACTH made by the pituitary gland with the gland no longer present. ACTH is a hormone sent to the adrenal glands as a signal to produce cortisol. With ACTH still present, my body continued to precipitate an excessive amount of cortisol while also being prescribed the hormone. We consulted once again with our physicians. Unfortunately, another surgery would be needed. The procedure would entail the removal of the adrenal glands responsible for the body's cortisol production and thus end the disease's effects.

The surgery was again performed at Jefferson University Hospital and was scheduled for January 2001. The adrenalectomy was to be accomplished using laparoscopic surgery. The surgery required more time than expected as the adrenals were severely enlarged due to being overstimulated for so many years. It was also thought that I had a third underdeveloped, nonfunctioning kidney. The aftereffects of the surgery lasted longer than I would have liked. I was stiff, bloated, and weak.

My health began to improve slowly with time. The hormone dosages were dialed into the correct levels. As I began to feel more like myself, I started to look forward to normalcy and a return to work.

Aftermath

Almost anyone who has suffered through a prolonged illness has experienced numerous questions and emotions. Why did this happen to me? What did I do to deserve this? Unhappiness takes hold and is able to thrive in this environment. Physical pain can also easily lead to a downward mental spiral. I had kindness, love, and prayers from family and friends. Their support was greatly appreciated and helped me overcome my troubles. This was also a time when I relied heavily on faith. If you trust in God and let Him in, you may perceive your adversity in a different light. Once I looked beyond my own troubles, I realized that innocent children had afflictions, and some would never recover. In truth, when you are able to look outside yourself, someone somewhere always has bigger problems than you. Trusting in God allowed me to frame the illness and my experiences in a positive light. Here are some of my conclusions:

- I am still here to tell this story, which means that God still has a plan for me. I can love my wife, children, and family for another day. I can use my skill set to serve others and, maybe, through conversation, offer hope and encourage faith.
- Because of my illness, Donna faced a lot of obstacles. She was responsible for our children, finances, and house. The depression that plagued her was left behind as she faced the new challenges caused by my situation.

- I received support, love, and prayers in abundance. I received cards and letters wishing me well. I received hugs from so many. I can say with certainty that when you are down, the simple act of a hug can lift you up, stick with you, and brighten the rest of your day. Have you hugged your plumber today?

- During the time of my illness and following, I passed the time by watercolor painting. This was something that I had wanted to do in my youth, and now the illness had given me the opportunity to pursue it. This craft fostered a creative outlet and allowed me to meet new friends and have new experiences. It allowed me to focus on the piece I was creating instead of my troubles. For a short time, my art was appreciated and purchased. It was displayed in several shops, and I participated in multiple art shows. On occasion, I am humbled to see them displayed in people's homes. I hope that I will have the opportunity to paint again.

Serenity

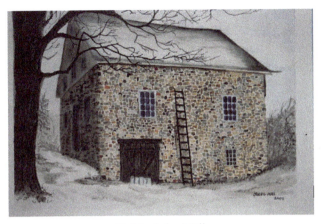

Behind the Mill

- Jefferson University Hospital is a teaching hospital. I was attended to by many fine aides, nurses, and doctors. I received excellent care. I was told that my case would be documented. It may assist in future treatments and may lead to the benefit of others. My illness impacted my daughter, prompting her to pursue a career in nursing.
- Most of all, it made me rely on my faith and brought me closer to God.

I could not say that I had fully regained my strength and stamina, but I felt the need to return to work. One of my earliest tasks as I tried to ease back into normal was replacing an effluent pump. The pump is placed in a tank following a septic tank to accept wastewater and transfer it to a drain field. Completing this job involved physically going down into the tank to assess and diagnose the problem. It was a confined space, and I stood in about six inches of water. There was an odor, and the residue from waste was on all surfaces. In the midst of all this unpleasantness, I looked up. The daylight shining through the tank opening was my only illumination. A feeling of thankfulness for God's mercy came over me. For months, I had worried if I could return to my work, unsure of my future. Yet here I was, in a place most foul, giving praise for the opportunity.

13

Gratitude

During the span of my illness, my business remained open and was operated by the capable hands of my brother-in-law, Troy. Without his dedication, I'm quite sure that I would have had no company to return to. As I gained strength and returned to work, I was thankful for the thoughtfulness and selflessness Troy displayed.

In approximately late July 2001, I was browsing the men's clothing section in Ames Department Store in Boyertown when I noticed a display for Dickies workwear promoting the American worker. The top prize was a new pickup truck. I tore off an entry without reading any further details. I waved it at Donna, telling her that I was going to win the truck for Troy. She laughed, telling me that I was ridiculous, and dismissed my plan. However, I was convinced that this was how I could express my gratitude for all that Troy had done.

We returned home, where I studied the details of the contest. Entries required writing an essay stating why your nomination should be voted American worker of the year. Further examination of contest rules revealed a midnight deadline for submissions, ending that current day. My resolve unshaken, I set about my task. My thoughts about all Troy had done translated into words easily as they had swirled in my head for months. I think I actually impressed Donna as I read the draft to her for critique. Email entries were allowed, so Donna typed and sent my submission. Life continued and the episode was filed in the back of my mind.

In late August, my phone rang. On the phone was a pleasant woman with a Southern accent. She explained that she represented Dickies and was calling to tell me that the contest's judges had been impressed with my essay. She went on to say that I hadn't won the top prize, but that prizes would be awarded to a finalist from each state. My submission would receive the prize for Pennsylvania. She also said that the story would be carried in some local newspapers. It was almost unbelievable. Imagine winning a place out of all entries received across the country. After all, what were the chances? Especially within twenty-four hours of the deadline. She went on to call Troy and explain his prizes and further details.

Weeks later, on September 11, 2001, our country and many lives changed forever. Troy received his prizes quietly through the parcel service, and most people never knew. I thought it was a story worth noting and contacted my friend Randy. He referred me to Jim, who worked for the *Boyertown Times*. Jim interviewed us and wrote a nice article that appeared in the paper along with a photo of Troy and me. I truly wanted to do something special for Troy. I hope, for a brief moment, my appreciation was made apparent.

Newspaper Photo

I Love Lucy

It was the summer of 1997. My father-in-law was recently widowed and was visibly lonely. After sharing twenty-five years of marriage with a woman he still clearly loved, how could one reach any other conclusion? We all were still dealing with the grief of her loss.

Since Mom's passing, Dad had tried to date, but nothing came of it. We often went out together for dinner or had him over to our house, sometimes spending the night. We were thankful for one another's company, but we were no substitute for the love he had lost.

I was working hard in my usual routine. I had a bathroom remodeling project scheduled through one of several general contractors I worked for. As I was just a subcontractor, I had not met or had any previous dealings with the homeowner. Everything went along as planned, and the homeowner was not present on the days I was scheduled to be there. My only company was a cocker spaniel who seemed very unhappy to be left alone. I was scheduled to complete the job on a Friday, and I don't believe I arrived until midafternoon. I quickly set about my task; valves were installed in the new vanity, and connections to the sink basin were completed. I assembled and set up the new toilet. I flushed it several times to water-test it and check for leaks. My final job was to install the seat and take care of some minor cleanup. I removed the seat from the box, only to find that it was cracked. Unfortunately, it seemed that the damaged location could provide a nasty pinch to one's posterior. As I completed my cleanup, the homeowner arrived, and I explained to her about the broken seat. By this time, it was after 5:00 p.m., and the plumbing supply had closed. I pledged to return the next day with a new seat. She was quite pleasant and very understanding. Something seemed very familiar about her, but I couldn't place where I may have known her from. We had a nice conversation prior to my departure.

Now I must admit, over the last few months, I had thought of helping find someone who might make a good companion for my father-in-law. I knew he had a lot to offer if he could only find the right person. At this point in time, there were no dating services. Where would someone aged fifty go to meet someone? Suddenly, I realized the obvious. Yes, of course, plumbing could bring two people together—amazing. So overnight, I tried to come up with something brilliant to say. It had been many years since I asked anyone on a date, and this would be the first time it would be on someone else's behalf. So the next morning, I promptly put my plan into motion.

I arrived at her residence armed with my wit and a toilet seat. We greeted one another, and I went about my first task. Ten minutes later, I was ready to implement phase two of my plan. As we started a new conversation, she told me to call her Lucy. As we spoke, she explained that she had recently been widowed. A bit further into our conversation, I realized the reason for her familiarity. Her husband was a teacher at my high school and had instructed me in driver's ed. During that same time, Lucy had been employed as the school nurse. I never had occasion to visit the nurse's office, but I do remember seeing Lucy in the halls. She would often smile, say hello, and be very pleasant. I even played soccer with her son, Michael, while a senior in high school. I went on to speak about my father-in-law and our family's recent loss. I proposed an invitation for dinner at our house where she could meet Dad and my family. She took my number and explained that she had a few affairs she was currently attending to. There was no promise, but Lucy told me she would consider it.

Weeks passed by, and I placed our conversation at the back of my mind. I believe I mentioned my exchange with Lucy to Donna but never mentioned anything to Dad. Some weeks later, to my surprise, I received a call from Lucy. She said that she would like to take me up on my previous invitation. We arranged a dinner for an upcoming Saturday evening. We explained the dinner invitation to Dad and prepared for the future gathering. Lucy arrived right on time, and I made all the introductions. Dinner ran a little later than anticipated. The conversation went great… between Lucy and me. We had plenty in common because of high school and familiarity, having lived in the Boyertown area. Dad seemed nervous and perhaps a little out of his element. At the end of the evening, they exchanged phone numbers, and I was cautiously optimistic. Some time passed, and they decided to meet without the accompaniment of chaperones. Dad did not go into detail, but he appeared to be more himself.

Over the next several months, I observed them becoming a couple, enjoying one another, laughing, and holding hands. Dad took on some of Lucy's favorite past times, tennis and golf. Always a competitor, he strived to improve himself. He excelled, as he had done with almost anything else I saw him do. Lucy shared compassion and support as I suffered through Cushing's disease. Both families grew closer and shared holiday occasions. Lucy decided to purchase a vacation house on the Jersey shore. Eventually an official announcement came. They intended to be married. The ceremony would be at their newly adopted church on the shore.

New Beginnings

They had a small but pleasant wedding with friends and family. Their nuptials were twenty-three years ago. They resided for a time in Boyertown, and eventually each of them sold their properties in Pennsylvania, buying a larger home at the beach and making New Jersey their permanent residence.

Our family grew once more, adding two new brothers and sisters. Our children once again had two complete sets of grandparents. We were invited for extended weekends. This allowed the kids to share time with their new cousins and experience life at the beach. Dad slowly made improvements to the new residence, making it their own. They have enjoyed traveling together to Great Britain, Europe, and domestically as well. They have done mission work through their church and have remained physically active. Lucy very much enjoys reading and needlepoint. Dad has taken up acrylic painting, participated in, and won several art shows. I have observed Lucy turn toward Dad as he says something amusing, and then they laugh. It is quite easy to see the affection and love they share pass between them. Lucy has given herself, her insight, and most of all love.

Mothers-in-law have long been disparaged in jokes by comedians for years. I have been blessed to have given and received love from two of the most wonderful women that have held the title.

Back in the Saddle

I purchased my first motorcycle around 1983, against my parents' wishes and advice. It was a used Yamaha 250. I had no prior riding experience. I applied for a learner's permit and eventually acquired my license. Owning a bike was somewhat of a novelty. Several friends rode, and it was inexpensive transportation. I mostly drove it to work, not so much for pleasure. When Donna and I started to date, we rode together numerous times. Prior to our wedding day, I sold it mainly for fear of anything happening to my future bride. The responsibilities of married life took over, and motorcycling didn't enter my mind again until 2005.

I had been through the ordeal of Cushing's disease, and the desire to be on two wheels emerged in its aftermath. Several friends were experienced riders, and I admired them and their machines. Our small town has a long history with motorcycles, as it is the home of the Reading Motorcycle Club. Each year, the town comes alive with the roar of bikes as the club hosts an annual anniversary celebration. The predominant brand of bike is the iconic Harley-Davidson. I had long realized that motorcycling was not the safest of sports, but still a strong desire to ride had been ignited. I discussed my feelings with Donna, and she offered no objections. I visited my local dealer, Classic Harley-Davidson, in Reading. I soon found and purchased a used 1995 Sportster model.

First Harley

The primary color was yellow, with brown stripping and tank badges. The previous owner had added numerous upgrades, and I was thrilled. Ownership granted me membership in a vast brotherhood, and I got my first wave from another rider as I cautiously drove it home. I drove solo for several weeks as I acclimated to my new machine. I signed up for a safety course to further sharpen my skills. Shortly thereafter, Donna rode with me, adding to my joy.

One day, we decided to visit the town of New Hope, located on the Delaware River just over forty miles from home. This would be our longest ride to date. It was a beautiful August day, and we walked around the various shops in town. Upon our arrival back home, Donna's discomfort was so great that she uttered the following, and I quote: "If you want me to ride with you, you need to get a bigger bike." I needed no further persuasion as trumpets sounded from above. Her request was practically akin to one of the commandments. Shortly thereafter, we returned to Classic Harley and traded the Sportster for a touring class model, the Road King. My new bike was a true beauty, glacier-white pearl paint with spoked wheels and chrome.

The Fabulous Road King

For many Harley owners, adding accessories is a big part of making the bike their own. As the thrill of riding and customizing my new bike took over, watercolor painting was soon left behind. Owning the bike opened many new avenues—riding regularly with old friends, making new ones, reaching overnight destinations and adventures, traveling an unknown road just to see where it might lead, and so on. I rode with friends through Pennsylvania and West Virginia. Another trip included the New England states, and when my daughter attended college in Indiana, I rode solo, covering Ohio, Indiana, and Southern Michigan.

One Sunday morning, Donna and I had planned on meeting Rebecca and Brandon for breakfast. The route we traveled included a large downhill slope, followed by an incline into a wooded area. I accelerated downhill to gather extra momentum and continued up the hill. As we climbed, a deer stepped out into the road and right into our path of travel. I had only seconds to plan any evasive maneuver. A car was moving toward us in the opposite lane, and the narrow road shoulder offered a bank strewn with large rocks, its angle sure to flip my bike. I applied the front and rear brakes hard, causing the bike to skid. The front of my bike struck the poor creature in her right hind quarter, turning her and sprawling her out. Her head struck Donna's leg as she slid across the road. We continued in our skid, coming to a halt upright at the very edge of the road.

A couple traveling in the car behind us stopped to make sure we were okay and offered their assistance. The gentleman exclaimed, "Man, I don't know how you did that!" I surveyed my bike, finding no damage other than the front fender being bent and pushed against the tire. The location was rural, but despite this, two separate police officers arrived on the scene, one heading for his shift and the other returning from his. No one had alerted them; it just timed out that way. They directed traffic safely around us and called for a tow truck.

While waiting, one officer told us, "You just don't walk away after striking a deer." The deer lay lifeless at the edge of the highway, and I felt bad for taking her life. The bike was towed home, and I removed the damaged fender and rode the bike to Classic Harley later that afternoon to order a new one.

In the days that followed, I had time to put more thought into the incident. My first thoughts were of how lucky we were. As I processed the event further, the comments from the driver behind us and the police officer played in my mind. I began to perceive that walking away had much more to do with God's grace and blessings than with luck. It was at this point that I was enlightened to a true awareness that God has a never-ending presence in my life. I was thankful that both my wife and I were left uninjured and realized, once again, that God's plan must still include me.

Husband and Father

I have been blessed to have fathered two children. At thirty-plus years of age, they still hug me, kiss me, and say, "I love you." This is of great comfort to me. I didn't regularly make that clear to my parents. It was an emotion assumed but most often left unspoken. I enjoy being in my children's company and now also spending time with my grandchildren. I am proud of both of my children and what they have achieved.

Our children grew up with our love and support in a home under a constant state of construction.

Daddy's little helper

Early photos portray them poking their heads through wall openings or wielding various hand tools. Donna always maintained a balance between being their mother and my helper. Of course, their grandparents were invaluable on many occasions, watching them and allowing us to focus on more intense projects. My daughter was quiet and reserved as a child. She never jumped directly into any situation. I can't remember ever having to yell at her. My son, on the other hand, was ready to try the next latest trend. He tested my patience on many occasions, and I am sure I yelled at him more than once. We celebrated birthdays and holidays. There were trips to amusement parks. We joined Cub Scouts and Girl Scouts. We tried soccer, swimming, and field hockey. There were overnight visits with friends, school memories, and summer vacation. And, of course, we attended church every week.

Looking back, I think we provided our kids with a pretty good degree of normalcy. My daughter struggled with her studies and mainstream learning. My son neglected his studies at any opportunity to have a good time. Eventually my daughter was placed into learning support. We, as parents, thought this would be a help to her. She began to hate this and wanted to be mainstreamed with the rest of the students. The school tried to discourage us from it. We soon became disillusioned with the public school system.

Rebecca desired to attend a Christian school and was even willing to put her small savings toward the tuition. Rebecca transferred to a Christian school in her ninth-grade year. We were so impressed by Rebecca's improvement in grades and demeanor that we sent Jules there as well, in his ninth-grade year. I don't remember Jules's grades improving much, but we felt he was in a much better environment. Rebecca participated in cheerleading, and Jules participated in soccer. They both made new friends and were involved in many extracurricular school activities. We never worried about our children using alcohol or drugs. When they told us they would be at a friend's house, we never worried that they were somewhere else. The new friends they had made were always respectful and polite. Donna and I have never regretted making that investment in our children's education.

Soon enough, the age of sixteen arrived. We taught the kids to drive, ensuring they both could operate a manual transmission, which I think is a life skill. Both children started to date; during these years, Rebecca attended a dance with one boy and returned home with Brandon, the boy she would marry. Jules achieved the rank of Eagle Scout, dated several girls, and hung out with friends. The school they attended annually arranged a college tour to visit the campuses of several Christian universities. Both of my children took advantage of this opportunity. Rebecca applied to Huntington University in Indiana. She had decided on a career in nursing, and the school had just instituted a program in that curriculum. This was her first ever extended time away from home. Donna and Rebecca have an excellent relationship, so the separation caused by college was not easy for either of them. Rebecca made new friends and adapted to her new surroundings and curriculum. She was truly dedicated to herself and her goals, even taking courses at a local college over her summer break.

Jules graduated from high school and was accepted at Philadelphia Biblical University, although his grade point average was lacking. He started college with a reduced course load and no declared major during his first two semesters. In his freshman year, he was treated for Viral spinal meningitis, leading to several stress-related seizures. He met a girl and began a serious relationship. In his sophomore year, Jules had the opportunity to visit Kenya on a mission trip. The experience deeply affected him and confirmed his desire to go into youth ministry.

Brandon asked for my permission to marry Rebecca and left for basic training in the Marine Corps shortly thereafter. Jules went through a very hard breakup and, for a short period, spent more time at home. He switched to a church he had previously attended, where he would meet his future wife, Adrianne. We attended Brandon's graduation from boot camp. The ceremony was very solemn and made me proud of him. He proposed to Rebecca that same day.

Brandon proposing to Becca at boot camp graduation

Life just got more complicated and expensive but in a good way. A date was set, and we started planning for our daughter's wedding. Later that year, I had the good fortune to work for a physician. His wife and I had a nice conversation, which, of course, involved the topic of our children. I explained that Rebecca was going to school for nursing. This chance meeting resulted in Rebecca having summer employment at his office and being hired per diem following her graduation leading to her current position. Rebecca graduated from college and got married to Brandon just weeks following. The ceremony was held at Washington Memorial Chapel in Valley Forge, located in the same park where I had proposed to Donna twenty-five years earlier.

Becca and Brandon on their wedding day Valley Forge Chapel

Jules worked as a youth director during an internship at a church in North Jersey. He graduated from college, worked on the maintenance staff at his church, and looked to go into youth ministry. Jules asked Adrianne to marry him, and they planned a wedding for the following year.

Jules and Adrianne Engagement

Soon after they married, Jules was offered a position as a youth pastor for a Bible fellowship in Sunbury, Pennsylvania. They moved to the area, rented an apartment, and, in a little over a year, purchased a home. They made many new friends through the church. They worked on their home, updating it and making it their own.

17

CHAPTER

Honor Thy Father

I was named after my father. When he was born, my grandmother had no name picked out; maybe a baby girl was expected. She named him after the doctor who delivered him.

I think my dad may have spent a lot of his growing up in his brother's shadow. I know little of his childhood, just small incidents and stories. One Christmas, he was forgotten, as all the gifts under the tree were tagged for his brother. I cannot even imagine how that must have felt. He had a speech impediment and was made fun of by other kids. I would say he was a bit of a loner. My grandmom once told me that after being chastised by others, he exclaimed, "Me play better by myself anyway!"

However, the man I knew was confident and proud. He often told me he would always be my best friend and lived up to that statement. Dad never once struck me for any infraction, choosing to talk instead. He once told me he felt that World War II was the nation's greatest time in history, as it solidly unified America. He felt our nation would never see anything close to that solidarity and commitment again. He loved my mother and proclaimed it to me often. He enjoyed being part of her family, especially in the company of his brothers-in-law.

My dad was closest to my uncle Albert; the two of them together were their own comedy team. The Abbott and Costello of the family, they shared the same sense of humor. They would just play off one another with a whole routine of jokes and laughs, completely unrehearsed.

Uncle Albert and Dad

He always talked to me like a man, asked me never to lie to him, defended me, and loved me. He was thrilled by the introduction of the VCR. He enjoyed movies about the West, war, and action. He loved music, from the big-band era to the Crooners to the Sound of Philadelphia. Sometimes he would march around the living room, moving his arm with an imaginary staff in hand, humming and singing, substituting his own lyrics, while my sister and I would march right behind him. I'm sure my affection for music and film started with him.

When we moved, he traveled daily for over an hour to and from Philadelphia for work, with the AM Top 40 radio being his only companion. We never played catch or threw a football together. Some Sundays, when Dad had time to sit, we watched war movies or comedies. Once he commented that one day he looked across the dinner table and noticed my sister was now sitting up and that I had grown to half a man. I guess many men have a *cats-in-the-cradle moment*. I know that I have. All my childhood, he had left for work before I awoke and never returned before 6:00 p.m. Sometimes he would come home, the phone would ring with an accident involving a telephone pole, and he would turn around and head right back to the city. He took all the overtime money he made and paid ahead on the mortgage.

Dad working - Line Man for Bell Telephone

He provided, worked hard, and was handy and resourceful. I learned a lot just by watching him in any task he performed. I was never discouraged from helping. He was fond of pointing a finger at his head and saying, "Once it's up here, nobody can take it away from you."

The job, over time, took a toll on his body. When he started as a lineman, the poles were climbed to service the wires. The work was hard and physical, and he was exposed to all the elements nature could dish out. Upon his arrival home, he would eat dinner, possibly watch an hour of television, and be in bed asleep by 9:00 p.m. I appreciated all he did, but I can't say that I grasped the full extent of what he stressed over and what he sacrificed daily to provide a home, clothes, and food for his family until I walked in his shoes. His advice was given freely, sometimes critical, sometimes good, sometimes bad, but always with love. He underwent numerous surgeries over the years. His spine was compromised, and several disks were removed. His body was worn and affecting his ability to work as a lineman. Eventually Dad got a transfer and spent his remaining years with the company in a position called a frameman. It was inside work and much closer to home. He made many new friends at the company office.

For all his hard work, he did eventually receive a retirement. He spent this well-earned time on home improvement and some travel with my mother, and he enjoyed more time with his children and grandchildren. Occasionally, he assisted us as we renovated and as I started my business. I know he longed to spend some time with me, but business ran me, so those moments were sparse. *We'll get together then, Dad.* Unfortunately, in time, his mind became clouded. Prior to his Alzheimer's becoming full-blown, my son and I made a compilation of photos from my parents' youth, courtship, and marriage. It included images of my sister, Sherri, and myself from birth to having our own families. This was then followed by each grandchild's birth to the current time. My son placed it on a disk and added music. We presented it to him and played the disk for the whole family on Christmas Eve of 2009. There wasn't a dry eye in the room as the memories of three generations flashed on the television screen. Unfortunately, the disease had already progressed too far, and he just didn't understand. I know this would have been his most treasured gift just years earlier.

My Father with Rebecca

I often think of my father. He set an example and laid a solid foundation for me to build upon. Certain places and songs conjure up the image of the man in my mind. Family gatherings now have a lot less color. I know he was proud of his family and proud of my accomplishments. I know I was proud to call him Dad and blessed to be his son.

Perpetual Motion

Life passes by quite quickly, and it waits for no one. While living it, dreams are realized, goals are reached, and loved ones are lost. Life will knock you down and laugh as you try to get back up. At the same time, you grow older while living in the moment. Before you realize it, you soon find your path altered.

Like a double-edged sword, work provides you with survival but can also be a burden. Being self-employed, the public's general perception is that you have wealth and can take a day off whenever you want; after all, you are your own boss. It all looks easy to those who have not juggled the balls. I had long felt I carried too much debt and struggled to keep up. I also found myself saddled with a tax problem. This resulted from a long list of my own mistakes, including a poor choice of an accountant. It was my burden to bear, and I kept moving forward, doing the work, making more bills, and pushing repeat. Motorcycling provided me with an outlet, a chance to focus my passion on the road and in that moment. It has provided and still provides a separation from my business, which seemed to encompass my entire existence.

My father had been diagnosed with Alzheimer's years earlier and was slowly slipping deeper into the dark void of the personal hell the disease provides. When death comes suddenly, it is a blessing from God. Although it is hard for loved ones left behind, it is much easier for the recipient. Watching a loved one wither, there is much time to wonder and contemplate their life and thoughts. There is more time to lose a bit of yourself. It was December 2012, just before Christmas. My father lay in a hospital room; all the family had arrived. We were told his time was short. He lay there, shrunken. His skin was pale and appeared gray, and he labored for every breath. This would be the last time I saw him, and it is a harsh memory I carry inside.

Christmas came, and still he lingered. Jules and Adrianne's wedding was planned for the twenty-ninth. It provided a much-needed day of happiness. My daughter-in-law was beautiful, and her bridesmaids wore red gowns. Unexpected snow arrived just prior to the wedding. It made their day all the more special, and the pictures of the wedding party in the snow were just beautiful. Just another blessing from God that I was able to witness.

Winter Blessing

They had picked a beautiful venue for the wedding reception. A sudden draft alerted me to a small dilemma. The backside of my rented tux had split down the seam. I spent the beginning of the affair, less pants in a cloakroom with Donna, our cousin Dorothy, and a borrowed needle and thread. I was irritated at first, but the girls' jokes and laughter soon changed my perspective. We enjoyed a good meal, seeing family, and time on the dance floor. The kids departed for their honeymoon, and my reality returned. Two days later, on a cold New Year's Eve, my father took his last breath with my mother at his side. And where was I? One might ask. I was working in the frigid darkness, trying to clear a blocked drain at a fire hall. Tears ran down my face after receiving the call. I could do nothing as my task was not yet completed. In a few short days, we celebrated a beginning and wrestled with an end. A lot was different.

The relationship I shared with Troy had also changed. After twenty years with him by my side, I had long come to depend on him, confide in him, and share many challenges of business together. It was all personal. My success was as much a reflection of his efforts as my own. Tension just seemed to float in the air around us whenever we shared a space. In 2013, Troy sat down to tell me he was taking a new position. It felt like I had driven head-on into a wall. I am sure it wasn't a decision he made without personal conflict. I understood his reasoning and knew it was probably best for both of us. Always a true gentleman, he gave me a full month's notice to process my thoughts and adjust my schedule.

The tax issue continued, and although we now had a competent accounting firm to guide us, the interest on the debt continued to accumulate. Any trip to the mailbox could make your heart sink into your stomach as you received the official correspondence. I leaned forward, knowing I had love and support from my wife and could depend on my faith in God to see it through. I told myself that these two things were constant no matter what life could throw my way. Life continued, and I learned to be more self-sufficient at work. I now had no one to call if a job went wrong, no one to run to pick up a needed part I may not have replaced on my truck. I learned to network with some other friends, and Troy still gave a hand when he was available. I worked a little longer and pushed myself a little further.

The year 2015 came on without much fanfare. Donna and I had been empty nesters for almost three years. I had traded my existing bike for a new one the previous fall, and I was ready to put some serious miles on it. At around the same time, I got Donna to start entertaining my two-wheel travel plans, and we went to dinner with Rebecca and Brandon. While at dinner, they handed me a gift. With no occasion in sight, I assumed it was missed or left over from Christmas. The box was small, about the size one might wrap a shirt in. I removed the wrapping and opened the box to reveal a toddler-size shirt with a Harley-Davidson insignia on it. I found myself a little lost as I did not grasp the intended message in the box. "Surprise, Mom and Dad. You're going to be grandparents." I was still wrestling with the fact that I had reached my fifties and wasn't quite ready to add "Grandpop" to my titles.

The winter soon melted into spring, and spring yielded to summer. Rebecca's pregnancy was progressing normally. Donna and I had planned a trip to Glacier National Park in Montana before and including the Fourth of July. It was a safe bet that the Going-to-the-Sun Road in the park would be open for travel by then. Rebecca was just starting her third trimester and was healthy and fit. She was having regular prenatal exams, taking her vitamins, and maintaining a healthy balance of exercise along with her job. Donna and Rebecca have always had a great mother-daughter relationship. They regularly converse, discussing thoughts, ideas, and the trials of daily life. Rebecca had, on several occasions, expressed worry that something was wrong. I dismissed this as nerves and told her she had no reason for dismay. You know, life can sometimes have a funny way of repeating itself. Brandon and Rebecca were living in a relatively new home in a development about forty minutes away. They collected antiques and really didn't care for their house or location. While pregnant, they had decided they wanted to be closer to the Oley area. It almost sounds like a story I heard somewhere twenty years earlier. Anyway, they actively looked for a new house, and we tagged along on several occasions for advice.

The date we had planned for our motorcycle epic adventure arrived, and we headed West for Montana. I was apprehensive as we set out, knowing, based on Donna's comfort and experience, this could be my first and last epic adventure...at least on two wheels. The first day went fine, and we made it to Indiana at about 8:00 p.m. Donna was tired but not saddle sore. We found a hotel, had a nice meal, and easily fell asleep for the evening. We arose for day two, and

I let the GPS be my guide. I had planned the trip loosely and hadn't determined a specific route. This resulted in a navigator error and an occasion to wear our rainsuits. The route took us past the steel mills in Gary, Indiana, and toward Chicago. I had no interest in seeing the windy city or being on a road that collected a toll for what seemed like every five miles. And for a little extra added bonus, the road was under construction. The rain made it all the more interesting, coming to a safe stop on the oil-soaked asphalt at each toll. The day wasted away, and we had only made it into Wisconsin under a tornado warning.

The next day was misty and damp, and we continued our route through Wisconsin and continued into Minnesota. The scenery was pleasant, but I was concerned about making it to Glacier and still making it home within the window of days we had allowed. My daughter still had her concerns with her pregnancy and continued to discuss them with Donna as we updated them on our travel progress. I was now ready to consult a map, plan my own way, and ditch the electronics. We traded 94-West for 90-West. We decided Glacier National Park would be too far of a stretch and set out for the Badlands of South Dakota. We spent the Fourth of July in Wall, South Dakota. We explored the Badlands, the Black Hills, Mount Rushmore, and the Crazy Horse Memorial. We trekked into Wyoming, visited Little Bighorn and the Devils Tower, and went over the Beartooth Pass. We touched on Yellowstone National Park and, after seeing the Mammoth Hot Springs, started back home.

Devil's Tower in Wyomming

The travel, new sights, and time spent alone with Donna were exciting and uplifted my soul. Upon our return, I looked forward to a future trip West.

I resumed my work, and the remainder of summer passed quickly. Rebecca grew more uncomfortable as her baby grew and more frustrated with the whole home-buying process; they had finally sold their house but had not made a settlement on the property they had purchased. And still, she worried about the health of her unborn child. I continued to assure her and teased that the baby would come out needing therapy.

Labor Day passed, and the baby's due date was just days away. Rebecca was admitted to the hospital with preeclampsia. Her doctor tried to induce her, but twenty-four hours had passed with no clear signs of delivery. Being a nurse, her mind naturally works in an analytical manner, so she quickly decided on a C-section after consulting with her doctor. Finally, on September 12, a baby boy arrived in the world. Everyone was happy and relieved that both mother and child were happy and healthy.

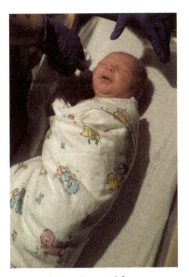

New Born Olyn

Newborn Olyn was passed from his parents to grandparents, aunts, and uncles. We left the hospital to let Rebecca rest and spend the remainder of the evening alone with Brandon and the new baby.

The next day, Sunday, Donna and I woke up and anticipated having breakfast and then heading to the hospital to visit when Donna's phone rang. It was Brandon, who was somewhat frantic, saying they had examined the baby and that something was wrong. We got dressed and headed to the hospital as quickly as we could. We were directed to a room along with Brandon's parents and brother. We were informed shortly thereafter that the baby was born with a heart issue and needed specialized care within the next twenty-four hours to survive. They said they were arranging transport by helicopter to a Philadelphia children's hospital.

Everyone was devastated; there were no words. How could this be? It was a living nightmare. There was a conflict with the transportation, and a specialized ambulance was dispatched. I felt overwhelmed and was overcome by a true sense of helplessness I had never experienced before. Once I choked back my tears, I prayed and prayed again. I prayed like I had never prayed before. I'm sure God listens to my prayers, but I am never sure that I am doing it right.

This was my only hope for my grandchild's survival, and there was no room for error.

God has always blessed me by putting firm, true believers in my path. When I say this, let me leave no doubt that I believe, truly, that the faith of the men and women I speak of cannot be shaken. So I proceeded to call or text them and ask for their prayers. Many of them added length to the chain by calling others. My friend Eddie wailed and wept and prayed like it was his child. Believers in foreign countries lifted their voices to God and prayed for Olyn. Within twenty-four hours, with her C-section still tender, my daughter was bouncing down the Schuylkill Expressway. Brandon and Rebecca spent the night at the children's hospital, sleeping on an intern's cot in a closet if they could sleep at all. Olyn had been born with arterial stenoses. A procedure was performed by entering the heart through the groin, and a transfusion was performed. My tiny, innocent grandson was covered in wires and connected to monitors and medications and was assigned to his own dedicated nurses.

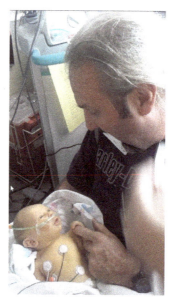

Olyn in hospital in Philadelphia

Over the next month, we traveled back and forth to the city numerous times. Rebecca and Brandon stayed at a Ronald McDonald house within walking distance of the hospital. They were at their child's side in an almost constant vigil. A blood infection complicated his recovery and prolonged his stay. Finally, after six weeks, he was stable and ready to come home. His heart was functioning, but not at 100 percent efficiency. His doctors were happy with his current heart health, but he would continue with appointments every six months. The procedures were temporary, and more invasive surgery would be needed as Olyn got older. We hoped he would outgrow the problem or, at the very least, technology would change and a miracle procedure would emerge. We were so thankful for his release and return home. Rebecca and Brandon made the settlement and moved their possessions from storage to their new address in Fleetwood, just over ten minutes away. We enjoyed our new grandson, and he grew just like any other child.

Meanwhile, as my daughter's life seemed to mirror ours, Brandon started the task of remodeling their new home. The next thing I knew, it was the week of Thanksgiving, and I had a full schedule. Christmas, with the expense it would bring, was around the corner. It is incredible how quickly each day's struggles can erode one's memory of God's most recent blessings.

It was a Tuesday evening, and I was way behind on the day's schedule. It was close to 4:30 p.m., and I still had a water conditioner to install. I could not push it into the following day as I was meeting my friend Rick to start an A/C installation. I cursed under my breath, as, along with being late, the installation was not going smoothly. I finished at about 7:30 p.m. and headed home, stopping for gas at the local convenience store so as not to run late the following morning. I made my gas purchase, and, just feeling down, I picked up a $20 Christmas-themed lottery ticket at the counter. A ticket that expensive was a stretch for me and out of character. I was not a regular player and had little faith in my odds of winning. My mind went to the expectation of a few thousand dollars and how it could help with the holidays. I headed home, and that quickly, the ticket and my aspirations were forgotten.

Donna and I headed to Boyertown for a bite to eat and returned home. Donna went to bed, and I sat at my desk, completing some paperwork. As I finished up in the office for the evening, I recalled my earlier purchase. I went outside to my van and retrieved the ticket. Without emotion, I scratched off the group of winning numbers at the top. I then proceeded to scratch off the top row. This revealed the number 37, corresponding with my winning numbers. I looked at the prize amount, and then I looked again. Under the number 37, the symbol "$1MILL" was present. This couldn't be real. I grabbed the ticket and ran up the stairs, screaming for Donna. She was already in twilight, as I turned on the light to exclaim my good fortune.

At first, she thought I was joking, having the same reaction I first had to what was in front of us. I made her look again and assured her that it couldn't be a joke. We cried together, knowing that the money could solve many of our problems, but that its amount could cause more problems as well. I didn't want my life to change, and I knew that could be a possible outcome if we were not careful. Paranoia set in as I worried about robbery and unwanted fame. I hid the ticket in a safe spot. The night passed, and I met up with Rick in the morning to start our next job. I attempted to go about my day as normal, but I didn't keep my secret long, and I shared my news with Rick. He gave me a joyful hug, sharing in my blessing, and I knew he would keep it to himself. We went about our work, and I must admit, I definitely had a pretty good attitude for the remainder of the day. I decided to share the news again with my close friend Linda, another true confidant. I am sure she was as shocked as I was and rejoiced at the news.

Thanksgiving arrived and we shared thanks with our family. Donna had taken Monday off, and together we took the ticket to a lottery office in Bethlehem. The lottery official was courteous as she processed and authenticated the ticket. After that, I was congratulated and asked if they could take my picture for the lottery website. I declined, explaining that I wanted to keep it private. The official said she understood and congratulated us again, and we left to return home. Everything seemed surreal, like a fog or a dream. Several weeks passed, and a trip to the mailbox revealed an official envelope from the lottery. Inside was a check for $750,000. That evening, Donna and I celebrated quietly together and rejoiced. The funds would take care of the immense burden of debt we had carried for years. We started slow, paying credit-card debt, the IRS, our vehicles, and then our mortgage.

It seemed we could breathe for the first time in a long time. We praised God for His blessings upon us. Our debt would have taken three lifetimes to repay, and its weight was constant, but with a single gift, everything changed. I have tried many times since then to win again, thinking it would be nice to retire and never worry about money again. All that exercise has revealed is the greatness of the gift. It has completely changed any conception of luck, chance, or fate. I am fully convinced it was given by God for the purpose for which it served. I never boasted about the winnings and only shared it with very few. Soon after, a local newspaper reporter somehow tracked me down, asking me to do a story on the event. She thought it would make an interesting story going into the Christmas season. Fortunately, she respected my wishes for privacy and dropped the inquiry. I have shared this account as I have no explanation or understanding of God's grace placed upon me. I can only express my true thankfulness for His blessings.

Be Fruitful and Multiply

As 2016 began, Donna and I could truly count our blessings. We enjoyed our new title as grandparents.

I set about helping Brandon and Becca with some remodeling. Jules and Adrianne continued in their contentment as they settled in with new friends and commitments. Soon thereafter, Rebecca announced she was pregnant and that the baby would arrive in October. The birth of our children was a year and two days apart. Rebecca's children would be separated by a year and just under two months. (History really does repeat itself). A little baby girl arrived that October, healthy with no complications. Brandon and Rebecca decided to name her after Donna's mother, Leoa Rose.

Leoa Rose

Jules and Adrianne became anxious to start a family as well. However, God had other plans in mind for them. Try as they might, they failed to conceive. They appealed to God in prayer and decided to adopt a child. They signed on with an agency and began several fundraisers to help reach the amount needed for adoption. I watched several times as case files were presented to them, raising their hopes and then great disappointment after being passed over. Yet they continued to be faithful. They had decided on an out-of-state adoption as some states were less costly than others.

Years passed, and finally, they switched agencies and received a case in Texas. A young mother had decided to give up her baby following the birth. Jules and Adrianne anxiously traveled to Texas for the birth of their newborn son. They named him after Adrianne's grandfather and his biological mother's grandfather, Anthony Jose. They spent several weeks in the state, seeing many sights and landmarks while waiting for all the legalities to be settled. Adrianne's parents, Jay and Maria, traveled to congratulate the kids and help with their new arrival. Upon their return home, they were congratulated by many family members as well as their church.

Months later, God blessed them with another amazing event. Through the church, Adrianne was told of a young unmarried couple with an infant daughter. The couple had split up, and the young father—God bless him—wanted to try to care for the child on his own. They became foster parents to young Genesis, who was only months younger than Anthony. Soon the father, with some counseling and persuasion from his parents, decided it was best for his daughter to allow them to adopt her.

Donna and I are the proud grandparents of four wonderful but very active and imaginative children, all under the age of seven. Little Genesis was not even a thought, and suddenly, she was a part of all our lives.

Anthony and Genesis

Anthony and Genesis interact and are as closely bonded as any other brother and sister. Once again, and in His own time, God has enriched my life and that of my children.

Our pride and joy

Connect the Dots

Growing up, falling in love, working, and having a growing relationship with God have connected me in so many ways to so many others. Life is a crossroads of acquaintances, events, and decisions that all intertwine. Simple kindness on the part of others has benefited me in ways that cannot be counted. The connections to others and how they came to be are both a miracle and a blessing.

Years ago, as I started out in business, Gene, the manager at Boyertown Supply, kindly referred me to his friend Pete. Pete then had me do several jobs at his residence. Pete owned a manufacturing business in Reading. He was planning some renovations there. He then asked me to work with his general contractor. His name was Rick. He worked hard, laughed and joked, and was always accommodating. We continued to work together, and it was always fun to be in his company. Rick was asked to help another contractor, Mark, on a large project. Rick recommended me to Mark for the required plumbing needs. I met the building owner, also named Pete, who continued to use me for future projects and passed my name to at least three other family members. I also returned to do future plumbing projects for Mark. Mark then referred me to his brothers, Jim and Duke, who have also since employed me on numerous occasions. Jim eventually went on to mention me to his friend, Dr. Steve. While doing a project for Dr. Steve, I was introduced to his wife Elizabeth. Our conversation on the topic of our children eventually led to my daughter's employment.

This narration spans thirty years. The light provided by three of the friends mentioned above has gone out but not the memories of their names, faces, or kindness. This is just but one example of many remarkable threads that I can reflect upon. In my favorite movie, *It's a Wonderful Life*, Clarence, the angel, says to George, "Strange, isn't it? Each man's life touches so many other lives." A fictional tale, yes, but every time I watch the film, I am lifted up as I ponder the picture's parallels that translate to real life. We are all blessed to be connected by our shared needs and commonality.

Life on Two Wheels

I am not sure where my fascination with motorcycles began. I spent a lot of time bicycling in my youth. Two wheels became my first mode of transportation, mobility, and freedom. I first rode upright without training wheels by being pushed down a neighbor's hill. One giant leap…I soon persuaded my parents to trade my first wheels, my old AMF bike, for a used five-speed with a banana seat and high handlebars. In my youth, Evel Knievel was a household name, and we all tried to emulate him—riding a wheelie, laying down rubber in a skid, racing and jumping ramps, even flipping and suffering my first broken bone, breaking an arm. One more blessing, just to have survived the foolishness of my folly. Eventually in the mid-seventies, the ten-speed bike became the latest trend, and my daredevil ways were left behind. Soon after, four wheels became a passion as I approached sixteen.

I picked up my first motorcycle, probably around age nineteen. It wasn't that much for fun or sport, just an inexpensive mode of transportation. With marriage and the responsibilities of a house and home, the motorcycle soon became a distant memory. Children came along and owning an older home with years of updating gave me plenty to do and think about. Maybe some new zest for life emerged from the ordeal of Cushing's. Maybe it could be called a midlife crisis. Maybe I needed a hobby other than work. Maybe it was the prestige of owning a Harley. Whatever called to me, once that spark ignited, I could not put it out.

My wonderful wife was most agreeable and consented to the purchase when I shared my desire with her. I have worked my way upward over the years through several models of bikes and have achieved complete satisfaction with my current machines. Riding can be as simple as a short trip for a bite to eat anywhere on a warm summer afternoon. Following a hard day's work, a ten-minute errand on the bike can change your whole mood, all drug-free. It is a fantastic way to live, see, and explore the country.

It sometimes grants you celebrity status. Children are often fascinated, and I watch their eyes follow us as we pass. Someone regularly walks up, no matter where you are, compliments your machine, and starts a conversation. In Yellowstone National Park, we had two separate requests from people visiting from both Italy and Japan for permission to take our picture. On another occasion, I made a gas stop and went inside to use the restroom. When I returned to our bike, I found Donna literally surrounded by a large group of folks from China on a bus tour. Rolling along on two wheels is a complete change of attitude.

I truly consider riding to be a spiritual experience, as all your senses are engaged. Your awareness of other vehicles, obstacles, and road hazards is heightened. The wind surrounds you as it rushes past your ears. The sun's warmth caresses your skin, and the occasional shade or a hollow provides a brief cool. The scent of pine, honeysuckle, and even fresh mountain air stimulates your nose. You experience all the beauty of God's creation. All these combine to give a feeling of calming serenity. Motorcycling gives you a chance to commune with old friends and make new ones on the road—an opportunity for fun and adventure, a release from the repetition of work and responsibilities, even if only for a brief moment of time. My bike has taken me to the Atlantic Ocean and West over a mountain pass, where snow still lay amid blooming wildflowers.

Beartooth Pass Montana

We stopped at locations and listened to the sound of silence. I had been soaked by the rain, stung by sleet, and chilled to my bones. I had taken roads just to see where they go and had followed the paths of native peoples and early settlers. The experience is almost akin to being a modern-day explorer. Although charted and mapped, the places we visited were all new and exciting to me. I had taken many photos, but they could not translate the wonder and beauty I have witnessed. My wife had accompanied me on most of these adventures and made them even more memorable.

The weather had finally turned warmer, and the first riding of the year had begun. I sat in the saddle and felt as comfortable as I was in my favorite chair. I hit the starter, and my machine came to life, the rumble of the mufflers like a melody. I rolled back on the throttle and head off down the road. I rode further only to realize I was one with my machine, and it was a reflection of myself and my personality. As I age, I prayed that I continue to retain the strength and skill needed to operate my bike and that new travels, sights, and friends await. I hope God will continue to offer us His grace, blessings, and protection as we ride.

On the Road and in God's Hands

It was a warm, sunny August day. Donna and I were on the eighth day of a two-week motorcycle cross-country trip. Earlier in our travels, we visited the Royal Gorge in Colorado, trekked across Utah, and traveled across Nevada on Route 50, designated on the map as America's loneliest road.

America's loneliest road

We then took in some of California, including Yosemite National Park. Our first day in Arizona we spent touring sections of Route 66 including the town of Oatman. On day 3, we had breakfast and had just left our hotel in the town of Page. Temperatures were expected to top out at around one hundred degrees. Today's itinerary was to visit the northern rim of the Grand Canyon. After the day's adventure, Donna and I planned on returning to our hotel and started our journey home the following day. We traveled Route 89 South through Navajo land. We stopped around noon to enjoy the sights of the old Navajo bridge across the Colorado River. After walking the bridge and taking some photos, we continued toward the canyon.

Navajo Bridge, Arizona

Following Alt. 89, the road climbed and twisted as we made our way to Route 67 in the town of Jacob Lake. The scenery quickly changed from arid and dry to lush and green, with high meadows, pines, and birch. The air was fresh, and it cooled us as the elevation continued to increase, heading toward the park entrance.

JULES J. HULL JR.

Entering Grand Canyon

We entered the park, anxious to take in the view. Seeing our first glimpse of the canyon, we felt eclipsed by its grandeur and natural beauty. I had dreamed of this visit since my youth, and the reality did not disappoint. We made our way along a trail, taking photos and enjoying the serenity. Reaching the trail's farthest point, we continued to marvel at God's creation.

After some time, we made our way back toward the parking area. Leaving the park, we decided to continue our travel on Alt. 89, toward Kanab, Utah. Twenty minutes into our journey, we entered a section of the Kanab National Forest that must have experienced a recent wildfire. We slowed our speed to forty miles per hour, as posted before a turn in the road. Seconds after exiting the turn, I shouted expletives as we crossed over multiple bans of tar applied to cracks in the road's surface. It felt as if we were on ice, as the tar prevented my tires from making any actual contact with the asphalt. The energy created from the rotation of the wheels was transferred upward throughout the bike's frame. My motorcycle handlebars shimmied uncontrollably in my hands as we left the road.

We continued across the rough terrain strewn with large rocks, bushes, and trees. All my strength and thoughts focused on keeping the bike upright. We continued toward some charred trees, their branches brittle and breaking as they contacted my helmet. The bike came to a stop, falling to the right. We lay in the dirt for a few seconds as the dust settled. My thoughts turned first to my wife as I gathered my senses. Making sure she was not injured, I started pulling my right leg out from under the bike. I exclaimed to Donna that I thought I had broken my ankle. As I stood myself up, I looked down to see that my right foot was turned left to a nine-o'clock position. That just didn't look right, so I reached down and turned it back to its correct location. By the time I had completed that, the first of several good Samaritans had arrived and handed me a bottle of water.

Someone called 911, and another calmed my wife. I was urged to sit down, and a woman helped me remove my boot while another emptied ice from her cooler into a pillowcase and placed it on my leg. Several sheriffs arrived, followed by EMTs and a fire crew. While one sheriff surveyed the scene and completed his report, I was accessed, and my leg was placed in a temporary splint. I stood up and placed my arms over the shoulders of the responders. With their assistance, I hobbled back toward the road and the waiting ambulance.

End of the road

With a little change in plans and our mode of transportation, we again headed for Kanab, Utah. My mind swirled as I processed all the hurdles suddenly placed in my path. We arrived at the hospital, and I was wheeled into an examination room. I was promptly attended to by a physician and several nurses. The ankle was x-rayed, revealing a break in the fibula. The physician explained that surgery would be needed for proper healing. We discussed options and decided that it would be best to travel home for the procedure. A splint was placed on the leg to stabilize it, and we were discharged. We sat in a lobby, waiting for our transportation to arrive so we could return to our hotel.

Donna and I discussed all that had occurred and all the implications of our current situation. We had no wheels (as if I could drive). We had no backup plan. Two thousand miles from home, in a splint, and on crutches. Then there was my work that started before our departure and obligations and promises. How could I take care of the needs of my clients? Let's not forget that bills never stop coming in. It didn't take long to figure out a plan. I gave it up and asked the Lord for help with the load. I called and texted friends, not to ask for pity, but for their prayers. Here I sit, surgery days behind me, my leg wrapped and elevated.

It was quiet as I ponder all that had happened in one short week. I thought of all the recent events that had positive outcomes in my favor. My motorcycle did not slide down the road or into the path of an oncoming car. We did not go over an embankment, which was numerous in the area. We could have bled or had internal injuries but not even a cut or scratch. We may have been paralyzed from striking the trees, but none of that happened. My wife suffered a significant sprain, and I had a broken ankle. Both are minor in the scope of what could have been. I have been given another day to take air into my lungs. I am here to recount this story. God offered His protection and blessed my wife and I once again...God may not have stopped the accident from happening, but He certainly controlled the outcome.

Blessings Abound

Let me start here by thanking the strangers who stopped and assisted us literally just seconds after the incident. Let me thank the sheriffs and emergency personnel who cared for us and generally dedicate their lives to the service of others, also the doctor, nurses, and staff at the Kanab Regional Hospital, where I received prompt and compassionate care. God bless you all.

Upon leaving the hospital, Donna and I discussed several options for a way to return home. We were AAA members, so we contacted the Reading, Pennsylvania, office and were connected to a wonderful agent named Rose. In short order, she arranged a rental car, hotel accommodation, airline tickets, and a chauffeured ride home from the airport. I cannot begin to explain the amount of burden that she lifted from us. We waited in the foyer area of the Page Regional Airport for our rental car to be pulled up to the curb.

We observed a woman sitting across from us weeping as she spoke on her phone. Donna and I both wondered silently why she was so troubled. We hadn't approached her when she finished her conversation and went into the restroom. I would assume to compose herself. Donna was crying quietly to herself, still quite emotional from all that had transpired. Suddenly, the same woman walked up to Donna and asked her if she was also in pain. She went on to explain that her son, only thirty years of age, was just found deceased in the bathroom by his child. She was at the airport trying to arrange a flight home. Suffering through all the pain of her devastating loss, she managed to show compassion for our situation. We exchanged hugs and promised to pray for one another as we parted company.

As we drove toward Flagstaff, we realized we were once again the recipients of another selfless act of kindness from a stranger. We hoped that in a way, we had offered her some small degree of comfort, as she had for us. The next morning, we made our way to Flagstaff Airport for a 6:00 a.m. departure to Denver. Once in Denver, on crutches, I was the sole participant in a one-man, three-legged race across the terminal to catch our next flight. Upon arriving in Philadelphia, I hobbled my way to the designated area to catch our ride home. Our driver was very courteous, and we made small talk across several subjects, finally ending up with a discussion on faith. The ride, which took more than an hour in rush-hour traffic, seemed like minutes as we shared many instances where God's presence in our lives was made clear. I can't help but think that God removed many hurdles and placed all these individuals in their place.

The eleventh day of our vacation started with a 9:00 a.m. visit to an orthopedist's office. My niece, Samantha, is employed with the practice as a radiology technician. She had prearranged my appointment two days earlier. We met with the physician's assistant, and she examined my leg, reviewed the X-rays, and rewrapped the ankle. She concurred with the diagnosis assessed in Utah. She explained that surgery was necessary if I hoped to be able to walk correctly again. Still in a heightened emotional state, Donna teared up.

I understood what had been explained and was prepared to face that reality. My only reservation stemmed from my fear of anesthesia. My father passed away years earlier due to dementia/Alzheimer's. My mother is currently dealing with memory and speech issues from vascular dementia. Both parents had consecutive surgical procedures prior to their diagnosis. I must say that it is my belief that anesthesia played a part in the equation. I had expressed my fears to my daughter, who is employed as a surgical nurse. She consulted with several anesthesiologist friends. It was suggested that spinal anesthesia would be my best option. However, years earlier, I underwent lithotripsy for kidney stones. The doctor at that time had me in tears as he attempted a spinal at least three times. He told me that if it was ever suggested for a future procedure, my spine was too thick for its success. Rebecca had great confidence in her friends' ability, and I decided to go in that direction.

We arrived at Reading Hospital for surgery at 6:00 a.m. the next day. Everyone was extremely helpful and kind, from the guard at the admittance desk to the nurses, doctors, and aids. Rebecca's friend, though not on the schedule came in special, just to administer the anesthesia. He introduced himself and went over the procedure. I was prepped, slipped into a fashionable hospital gown, and wheeled to the operating room. I sat up on the table and leaned forward, preparing for the doctor to administer the spinal. A nurse stood in front of me, and I held her hands. I cannot begin to explain the feeling of comfort she gave me in that simple act. There was some discomfort as the needle entered my back, but there was no need for a second attempt. The surgery went well, and I awoke in the recovery room. Once again, another nurse transferred calm and compassion through a hug. The title of healer does not begin to encompass the power of kindness freely displayed through the profession they have pursued.

I once again contemplated a reason for my situation. There was no way for me to rush my recovery. God always has a plan. I turned to look for something positive. I decided that I had been given an opportunity. The accounts I have provided on these pages are a result of my labor during my recuperation.

In the weeks following my surgery, I received cards, phone calls, meals, and visits. Still others offered very generous monetary gifts. In truth, I received one visit or call each day for a full month. There is healing that comes along with the well-wishes and prayers from others. I soon realized the depth and complexity of the many friendships I have been privileged to be a part of. Some men measure their success by their physical possessions or wealth. True wealth is measured by knowing your friends are willing to lift you up in a time of need. One such time, a very special friend, Eddie, arrived here with his Bible in hand. He wept as he prayed for us, despite the recent passing of his beautiful wife. I hope to someday achieve the strength and conviction of faith at that level. I have all this love and support from so many from all backgrounds, and the commonality that binds us all together is faith.

A Mother's Love

For most, a mother's touch is the first thing they will remember. A protector, always there to lend comfort, advice, calm, and most of all, love. She has her own gallery filled with your arts and crafts. She fixes the scrapes and scratches and makes it all better. Mothers work hard to raise us, asking little in return. She is the matriarch of the family and the glue that holds it all together. My mother is all this and much more.

Early in my life, I spent much more time with her than with my father, and for most of my first six years, I was the focus of her attention and affection. She was the first woman I ever loved. As I grew older, things began to change. I remember the first extracurricular activities my mother participated in; she bowled and joined a ceramics class. Her ceramics adorned our home during each holiday. For a time, she played volleyball. Eventually, she became involved with a local Girl Scout troop, becoming the leader. Meetings, campouts, and related undertakings filled up her time. Following that, she started to referee girls' field hockey. Soon after, she also officiated girls' lacrosse and basketball. She worked hard at her rating, starting in junior varsity, followed by the varsity, and then leading into collegiate, and tournament play for all three sports. She loved her craft and was completely dedicated.

It seemed to me that most of her focus had shifted to athletics. Often no one was waiting for me when I arrived home at the end of the school day. Mom was off on the field, court, or in attendance at some associated meeting. Dad often prepared dinner for my sister and me. I never felt as if I wasn't loved, but I must admit, I carried some resentment. Her "games," as she called them, seemed to hold much greater importance to her than her family. She was also the disciplinarian in the household. I often thought her punishments and groundings to be much more severe than any committed infraction. I was happy for every opportunity to be with my friends. When I was able to drive and started to date, I was happy for that time away from home as well. I continued to blaze my own trails. I was delighted to marry Donna and have our own house and home. I was sure of what I desired from my love and marriage. I continued to have a "you go your way, I'll go mine" attitude toward my mother for most of my adult life. It seemed everything revolved around her sports schedule; she was often late for grandchildren's birthdays and other family occasions.

Mom with one year old Rebecca

However, after many years, I came to realize that when Mom was needed the most, she was there, right up front, taking the lead. During the birth of our children, she was right by our side. When

Donna and I got so sick with the flu that we could not function, one simple phone call and Mom came over, with not a second thought for her own well-being. When I underwent surgery for Cushing's disease, she was right by Donna's side, supporting her and calming her fears. Always thoughtful, a significant portion of the money Mom made officiating, she used to treat her family out to dinner. Clothes and presents on any occasion for her grandkids were taken care of. Mom always placed a generous amount in a card for birthdays, Christmas, and our anniversary. Her gifts were always appreciated and always a huge help.

I am sure this was mirrored for my sister's family as well. There are countless other examples of her love and kindness to her family. She also went over and above to help her friends. Her love was not shown so much through words but through her many selfless acts of kindness. I watched her age as she struggled as the principal caregiver through my father's long battle with Alzheimer's. At his memorial service, I observed a long line far beyond the funeral home's entrance. Strangers to me, many in attendance; friends whose lives she had touched gathered to offer condolences and support for my mother—a true tribute to her impact on others. I watched her mourn the loss of her husband and continue to wear her wedding band and my father's as well.

Following my father's passing, we spent much more time together, not wanting her to feel isolated or alone. She remained very active and continued to officiate into her mid-seventies. Mom was inducted into several halls of fame for her dedication and skill in her profession. I am approached regularly with a memory or well wishes from someone who shared an association with Mom.

Several years ago, she was diagnosed with vascular dementia. This, of course, was life-changing and extremely upsetting for her and all those who loved her. There is no treatment or cure, and the family offered her support and encouragement. We assured her our love for her would not change and tried to help her with her thoughts when her words failed to form. She resided with Troy and Sherri for a time, eventually becoming stubborn and belligerent. Soon incidents with the stove or a hot shower running for hours occurred. After some discussion, it was decided that Mom could no longer be left unsupervised. The family gathered and cleaned out the home that she and my father had built. Old memories resurfaced, and all were saddened. Cherished items and possessions that made up their lives and ours were dispersed, sold, or just given away.

She is now residing in a memory care facility, most days lying in bed, no longer able to communicate, trapped inside a body with a mind that no longer functions. I am saddened once again to be a witness to a parent suffering the pain of lost words and memories. I had hoped for a more dignified ending for my mother. We often joked that she would have a massive heart attack while on the playing field and expire in glory doing something she loved. I am blessed to call her my mother, and I'm thankful for the additional moments we have shared since my father's passing. The resentment I held for her is long gone, and I now realize that the "games" she so loved were her "motorcycle."

Marilyn Hull
October 8, 1941–March 27, 2023

The Final Chapter

With no experience in penmanship, I have managed to write this brief history of true events that have happened to me while on this path called life. In my younger years, I had no clear expectations of what my life would be or where it would lead. My main objective as a young man was to find my true love, followed by survival. My life experiences have passed by ever so quickly. I am approaching my sixtieth year, and no matter how you slice it, my journey is more than half over.

I am thankful for all of God's guidance and blessings. I am thankful for the kindness and love shown by the many people I have met. It has been my honor to think and speak freely. I don't expect to find a nomination for sainthood in the mailbox anytime soon. I have fallen many times, and it has been made quite evident that my God has helped me up. I have made many mistakes and done things I have no pride in. I am a poor example of a Christian; I cannot even quote scripture. I am quick to anger, and I sin daily. I curse too much, often taking my Lord's name in vain. I keep trying to get it right. I attempt to follow His commandments, and when I fail, I ask for His help and forgiveness. I pray for others and give thanks for the blessings I have been given. My cup runneth over.

It has become ever so obvious that I am just an ordinary man with an extraordinary God.

I look down at my hands. They are scarred and callused, but they have done honest work. I have served others with my knowledge, skills, and ability. I often reflect while traveling down any given road, as I pass the numerous households where I have played a part in some repair or project. I enjoy my job not only because it allows me to help others but also because it allows me to share bits of myself, my opinions, and my faith. I have learned that everyone has a story, and you can learn much by just taking the time to listen. I have made new friends, and many have shared events in their lives and have extended kindness. My worries have often haunted me; I have contemplated scenarios and outcomes which have never come to pass. I realize that money is just a tool, a means to provide. It is not to be treasured or to be the focus of our lives. With age, I have come to appreciate the free time and quiet moments more, even the simple ticking of a clock. With the passing of time, I have gained a greater perception of what is real and truly important. I have a clear understanding of good and evil, what I can control, and what controls me.

I am so truly thankful for my best friend, my wife, Donna. She is the greatest blessing in my life, and I can't imagine being without her. She is the cooler head between us, and the understanding, love, and wisdom she has offered me are the main ingredients of any success I have come to know. Donna has long been my inspiration. She has given true meaning to the vows "in sickness and in health." We are not only connected by faith, marriage, and family; she is part of my soul. We can complete each other's sentences and often know what the other is thinking. She is, in all ways, my heart's desire. I pray that God has plans for us to be together for many more years.

I enjoy the time spent with my children and my grandchildren. My children's drive and their accomplishments are a wonder to me. I am proud of them. They have strived to help others, and Christ is always their guide. My grandchildren are exhausting, an endless power source from dawn to dusk. I ponder their parents' ability to keep up with them. I enjoy their new discoveries and their innocent observations and comments. We know our eldest grandson, Olyn, will reach a time when he needs surgery on his heart. I have already contacted many in advance for their prayers. As I began to edit my original writing, Olyn's physicians reviewed his case and decided to delay any procedure for now. They hope to wait until he is ten years of age when his heart stops growing. After age ten, a third additional procedure would not be required. Maybe technology will advance, and his procedure may be less invasive. I just see this new development as another blessing from our God above.

I do not involve myself in the things many others thrive upon. I do not spread rumors, and I don't carry tales. Gaming, social media, and cell phones do not hold any interest to me. I very much enjoy music, and I do have a device, filled with my favorites. It is a large collection with a mixed genre. It contains songs I enjoyed in my youth and songs that I find speak to my life experiences. Some rock, some make me reminisce, and others lift me up and make me think of my Lord. Many cast visions in my mind of my wife and the love we share. Mostly left to my tasks and my solitude, the music makes the day go a little faster and a little smoother.

I do not obsess over fear. Life so far has challenged me, taught me, and shaped me. When death comes, I will accept it willingly, satisfied with all that God has provided. I am imperfect, and I hope all my good deeds will outweigh all the bad. I hope my God will let me pass through to His kingdom so that I will once again be reunited with loved ones who have already made that journey. Tears dropped upon these pages as I recounted my days and experiences, some happy and some sad. I realize that God has provided everything I ever needed, and I have been given possession of true happiness.

Faith is acquired and built over a lifetime, and I am pleased that God has enabled me to impart and share all the memories and impressions that have swirled around in my mind. They are all true; nothing is stretched or fabricated. It is the entirety of my life up to this moment. I did not start this undertaking looking to make or leave a mark. Perhaps people will find it interesting, or maybe it may make others recount their blessings. It will, at the very least, be a family history. I hope it does, however, give glory to God and that it catalogs a moment and shares the blessings afforded a common man.

Each person is unique. Everyone has an amazing story to share. All can find God's blessings present in their lives.

Feel free to make use of the next few pages and document a blessing or something special about yourself. When we pass, so do our memories and experiences. It is the only thing we will truly take with us. Unrecorded recollections are lost to time. Share your thoughts and words with a friend, family member, or even a stranger. Record a small moment in time. You may be surprised to find you have encouraged or helped another.

Isn't that really why we are here?

About the Author

 Jules J. Hull Jr. is a son born to middle-class parents, each with individuality and perspective. Placed near the end of a generation categorized as "the baby boomers," he arrived shortly into the turbulent '60s. As a young child, he had few actual responsibilities. Watching his parents and grandparents as they interacted and worked taught him many skills and lessons, others he learned through imitation. In youth he cut grass and shoveled snow, soon understanding the concept of work and reward. He has always been fascinated by nature and took interest in insects and animals while growing up.

While attending school he was considered an average student, choosing to focus on topics and subjects he found interesting. He was fortunate to comprehend and enjoy reading. He appreciates both the written word and song. Jules's parents, their neighbors, and friends mostly had blue-collar roots. Knowing self-responsibility was expected he pursued the skilled trade of plumbing. Earning the title of a master plumber, it is no surprise to find him still using his hands in his chosen vocation.

Creativity has always been a gift present in his life. Art was a distant memory until illness allowed it to surface once more. Mostly self-taught, he enjoys the medium of watercolor—his subject, most often rural barns and scenery present in the Oley Valley. He feels fortunate to be able to express himself through painting.

An avid motorcycle enthusiast, he has traveled roads on two wheels in forty-one of the nation's states. He has a true passion for the adventure of a journey. He is a loving husband, father, and grandfather. His family, time spent in church, and personal relationships with many believers have helped in shaping his faith. He has realized the abundance of gifts and love God has shared. He felt called upon to write and has a lifetime of love, faith, and experience from which to draw and to reflect fondly. He completed this memoir not to boast but to share the true grace and blessings of God.

Printed in the USA
CPSIA information can be obtained
at www.ICGtesting.com
JSHW070028061023
49388JS00005B/7